The Word Proclaimed

· · · · · · · · · · · · · · · ·

A Homily for Every Sunday of the Year

Year A

William J. Byron, SJ

Paulist Press
New York / Mahwah, NJ

Cover image credits: Black background art by Lucy Baldwin / Shutterstock.com. Red background art by Eky Studio / Shutterstock.com. All rights reserved.
Cover design by Sharyn Banks
Book design by Lynn Else

Library of Congress Control Number: 2013952667

ISBN: 978-0-8091-4810-3 (paperback)
ISBN: 978-1-58768-291-9 (e-book)

Published by Paulist Press
997 Macarthur Boulevard
Mahwah, New Jersey 07430

www.paulistpress.com

Printed and bound in the
United States of America

Contents

Dedicated to
The Faith Community
at
Holy Trinity Catholic Church
Georgetown,
Washington, DC

Introduction

This is a book without a theme, unless the liturgical calendar can be said to provide a seasons-of-the-year theme for the Sunday homily. It is, however, a book based on a theory—a theory of the homily—namely, that every homily should be an extension of the proclamation. This is the liturgical principle that underlies every chapter in this book and its two companion volumes that complete the coverage of Years A, B, and C of readings in the Sunday lectionary.

Sacred Scripture from Old and New Testament is proclaimed in the first part of every Eucharistic liturgy. The homilist then extends the proclamation by filtering it through his or her own faith experience and tries to match it up with the faith experience of the people in the pews. That is always a challenge; but being mindful of the challenge to extend the proclamation in this way provides the homilist with direction in rendering this service to the people of God. Homilists have a personal responsibility to heed and incorporate into their own style of delivery these words from the pen of St. Augustine: "[I]f I speak to someone without feeling, he does not understand what I am saying" (from a *Treatise on John*, Tract 26).

We are a Sunday people, we Catholic Christians. We gather in Eucharistic assemblies every Sunday to remember the Lord in the breaking of the bread. In this way we give praise and thanks to God. That is our Sunday obligation—to give thanks to God. We thus declare ourselves to be "much obliged"—to be grateful, and we express that gratitude in praise of God and love of neighbor. Gratitude is the foundation of our religious observance. It is in gratitude that we gather to hear the word and share in the breaking of the bread. Nourished every Sunday by both word and sacrament, we go forth each week to serve our neighbor.

We break open the Scriptures in our Sunday assemblies where we find Christ present not only in (1) the Eucharistic elements, (2) the faithful who are gathered there, and (3) the person of the priest-presider, but also

(4) the proclamation of the word and in the homily. A well-prepared homily is filtered first through the faith experience of the homilist and, so far as possible, matched up to meet the faith experience of the faithful in the pews. Somehow, Christ is there in both pulpit and pew.

This book is a collection of one homilist's efforts to extend the proclamation in ways that will touch the hearts and minds of believers. Every chapter in this book is a delivered homily. They've been road tested in parishes and university chapels. They've been preached, heard, reflected upon, and discussed. Standing alone as a book, apart from any liturgical setting, this collection might prove helpful (if taken just one homily at a time) to people in any parish community. On the desks of priests and deacons, this book could serve as a source of ideas for extending the proclamation and matching it to the faith experience of those the homilists are privileged to serve.

To the extent that this book proves useful to the occupant of any pulpit or pew, or to any reader interested in reflecting on God's word in quiet moments apart from the crowd, my purpose in putting it together will have been achieved.

I've heard it remarked recently by a disaffected and discouraged Catholic worshipper that in the United States we have "*Saturday Night Live* and Sunday morning dead." I hope this book can help to change that. I've also heard from a pastor who hosted a foreign pastor during a visit to this country that his guest commented to him: "I notice that in your churches the benches and kneelers have cushions; I've noticed that your homilies are usually cushioned too." Perhaps the to-the-point style of the homilies offered here will facilitate the discovery of both challenge and encouragement in the word proclaimed, the word explained, and the word received. My message to the reader is an expression of hope, borrowed from Paul's First Letter to the Thessalonians (2:13); it is simply this: "that in receiving the word of God from hearing us, you received not a human word but, as it truly is, the word of God, which is now at work in you who believe."

—*W.J.B.*

I
Advent

. . . .

1

First Sunday of Advent

Isaiah, 2:1–5; Psalm 122; Romans 13:11–14; Matthew 24:37–44

THE SPIRIT OF ADVENT EXPECTANCY

The question to be asked each year on the First Sunday of Advent is this: Do you conduct yourself during Advent in a spirit of "make-believe," or in a state of genuine expectancy?

If it is something real that you will experience spiritually in these next four weeks, then someone really is coming, something real is about to happen. You are not about to enter into an exercise of make-believe; you are entering a stage of enthusiastic expectation. Only if something real is beginning today can you carry the reality of Advent expectation in your heart over the next four weeks.

How can it be real? Christ has, in fact, come. Redemption has in fact occurred. These events cannot—really, historically—happen again. Is Advent make-believe, after all? The coming of Christ and the redemptive work of Christ are ongoing realities, but they can only be real now, in this calendar year, if they occur in human hearts, if they happen in you and me.

This means that the entire mystery can be renewed now and extended in you, if you let that happen. It means that the entire mystery can be consciously appreciated now in you, if you let that happen. You can, if you will, live it all again. You can now, more than ever before, let Advent reflection help your soul to appreciate and appropriate the mystery of Christ's coming to you, to rescue you from darkness, to save you from your sins. And not you only, of course, but the entire world!

The spirit of Advent expectancy: Cultivate it in the spirit of the closing words of today's Gospel message: "So too, you also must be prepared, for at an hour you do not expect, the Son of Man will come."

3

Take those words not as a threat, but as a promise—a reassuring promise of safety, salvation, victory, of light out of your present darkness.

Cultivate the spirit of Advent expectancy in the spirit of the opening words of today's second reading, the selection from St. Paul's Letter to the Romans: "Brothers and Sisters: You know the time; it is the hour now for you to awake from sleep. For our salvation is nearer now than when we first believed; the night is advanced, the day is at hand." In other words, wake up! You have work to do.

Cultivate the spirit of Advent expectancy in the spirit of the stirring words of the Prophet Isaiah, repeated for you today in the first reading: "Come, let us climb the Lord's mountain, to the house of the God of Jacob, that he may instruct us in his ways, and we may walk in his paths." Let that be your Advent program. Position yourself through prayer and reading to be instructed once again is his ways. It won't happen against your will. You have to want it to happen. You have to let it happen. You have to pick up the book. You have to take time out for prayer.

In moments of Advent reflection check to see whether or not you are walking in his ways. If you are, perhaps you should pick up the pace, walk a bit faster. If you are not, then consider how best to reposition yourself so that you may "walk in his paths."

Many centuries ago, those who took the instruction to which Isaiah refers, "beat their swords into ploughshares and their spears into pruning hooks." What might we find ourselves doing now in modern times if we choose to "walk in the light of the Lord?" How might our swords be beaten into plowshares? How might our spears be converted to pruning hooks? How might we feed the hungry and help the hungry feed themselves in a secure world worthy to receive the Prince of Peace?

Isaiah had it right then and it remains right on the mark today: "Come, let us climb the Lord's mountain!" There is a mountain of resistance to be climbed. A mountain of fear and hatred to be overcome. A mountain of misunderstanding is out there in front of us. If Advent is to be something real for us this year, and not just a make-believe exercise, we have to work now to overcome those mountains in ourselves, and work together to overcome those mountains that stand as obstacles in our modern world to the coming of the reign of Christ.

4

To make all of this very real for us this year, see if Paul could possibly be speaking in any way to you with the same words you heard him speak to the Romans: "Let us throw off the works of darkness and put on the armor of light; let us conduct ourselves properly as in the day, not in orgies and drunkenness, not in promiscuity and lust, not in rivalry and jealousy. But put on the Lord Jesus Christ, and make no provision for the desires of the flesh."

Tough words; tough times—what is God calling you to do this year to make the Advent experience real in your life?

2

Second Sunday of Advent

Isaiah 11:1–10; Psalm 72; Romans 15:4–9; Matthew 3:1–12

REPENT, FOR THE KINGDOM OF GOD IS AT HAND!

On this, the Second Sunday of Advent, we meet John the Baptist, a strong and central figure in our Advent liturgies, who, as Matthew's Gospel describes him, "appeared preaching in the desert of Judea and saying, 'Repent, for the kingdom of heaven is at hand!'"

Meet John the Baptist once again this morning. See him, an imposing figure who "wore clothing made of camel's hair and had a leather belt around his waist." Hear him say to you this Advent message: "Repent, for the kingdom of heaven is at hand!"

This is the first of three points I want to lift up for your consideration from today's Gospel reading. All three are Advent points. All three relate to your participation in the Advent exercise of preparing, as John the Baptist did, the way of the Lord—the way of the Lord again this year into your own heart, and the way of the Lord into our modern world, a world Christ came to rescue, a world he came to lead from darkness into light.

"Repent, for the kingdom of heaven is at hand!" For political and practical reasons, Matthew does not say "kingdom of God." However, his expression, "kingdom of heaven," less likely to offend the religious sensibilities of his Jewish readers, amounts to the exact same thing—the reign of God, the dominion of God over human hearts and minds, the alignment of human wills with the divine will—the kingdom of God. That kingdom, says John the Baptist, is now "at hand."

It is interesting to note that in the first chapter of St. Mark's Gospel, you have an account of the beginning of the Galilean ministry of Jesus that opens with these words: "After John had been arrested, Jesus came

to Galilee proclaiming the gospel of God: 'This is the time of fulfillment. The kingdom of God is at hand. Repent, and believe in the
gospel.'"

Repent. Believe the Gospel. The kingdom—that is, God's reign over
human hearts and minds—is "at hand." Apparently, the kingdom has
been "at hand" now for two thousand years, but not yet fully grasped.
Why? Because the repentance, the *metanoia*, the change of heart, the
attitudinal turnaround, the value reversal that Jesus demands of us,
has not taken place. That should be our concern—personally, nationally, and internationally—in this Advent season.

Take another look at John the Baptist—a radically free man, a committed man, a man on a mission: to prepare the way of the Lord. That
mission could not be encumbered or compromised by the things of
this world, by comforts or commitments that could distract him from
his mission. Matthew says that, "Jerusalem, all Judea, and the whole
region around the Jordan were going out to him [John] and were being
baptized by him," by this man on a mission who wore simple garb and
ate locusts and wild honey. Don't be frightened by John the Baptist.
Just listen to his call to repentance. And note his further instruction,
words of John that I highlight for you now as point number two.

John said, as he noticed the Pharisees and Sadducees joining the
crowd, "Produce good fruit as evidence of your repentance." Produce
good fruit. Take those words to heart, dear friends, in these days and
weeks of Advent. Produce good fruit. Think about that personally, of
course, and attend to anything the Lord might be asking of you in the
way of personal repentance and the production, personally, of good
fruit. But think of the application of this mandate on a broader scale.
Think of it nationally and internationally. And, indeed, dare to think
of it in the context of the problem that is on all our minds, the problem
of what some are calling a "third world war," or, as Thomas Friedman,
phrased it in a *New York Times* column (November 27, 2001), a war
against "religious totalitarianism." This is the "real war" we are facing
now, said Friedman. Not a war against terrorism, but a war against
religious totalitarianism. Terrorism is just a tool, a weapon; religious
totalitarianism is the enemy, just as secular totalitarianism, Nazism

and Communism, were our enemies in World War II and the Cold War.

If you are to produce "good fruit as evidence of your repentance," you should give some thought to how tolerant you are of other faiths, how respectful you are of the way others might approach your one God. You might hope and indeed pray that others follow the approach that you believe is best, but you must respect their religious freedom.

Your own Catholic religion has had its excesses in the past, its "holy wars," its use of violence against "infidels." We have struggled with this for centuries before coming to a maturity wherein we are comfortable with modernity, wherein we acknowledge and accept religious pluralism. In the middle of the twentieth century, the Catholic Church, largely through the work of the American Jesuit theologian John Courtney Murray, produced in the Second Vatican Council the "good fruit" that is the famous Declaration on Religious Freedom. We repented of our earlier excesses, as Pope John Paul II had the courage during his pontificate to express public repentance for past sins of intolerance and persecution of those who did not share our beliefs. We have to think about that now and pray—pray that from within Islam an intelligent and devout Muslim mind will emerge to articulate a doctrine of religious freedom that will displace the false and destructive beliefs that distort Islamic doctrine and drive religious fundamentalist fanatics to use terrorist tactics to destroy us whom they regard as "infidels."

We must regard them as brothers, Muslim brothers and sisters, with whom we share the one God, who is a God of love. Our Christ requires of us that we love our enemies. May that love bear fruit in prayer. And may that prayer, in turn, produce fruit in the form of an enlightened acceptance, on the part of those whose minds are now trapped in the grip of religious fundamentalism, acceptance of the fact of religious difference in our modern world. May those who hate us see in us evidence, some "good fruit," if you will, that is rooted in a God whom we know to be a God of love.

My third point is to restate the words of John: "Every tree that does not bear good fruit will be cut down and thrown into the fire."

The stakes are high. Our responsibility to learn about, to grow in love of, and to respect the religious traditions of those whom we might all too easily dismiss as "infidels." We have a responsibility to understand the historic and religious roots of the tensions we now experience between Christianity and Islam.

Let me close with a brief quotation from the Friedman article: "Although there is a deep moral impulse in Islam for justice, charity and compassion, Islam has not developed a dominant religious philosophy that allows equal recognition of alternative faith communities. Bin Laden reflects the most extreme version of that exclusivity, and he hit us in the face with it on 9/11." In effect, Friedman is saying that Islam has not yet produced a John Courtney Murray.

- "Repent, for the kingdom of heaven is at hand!"
- "Produce good fruit as evidence of your repentance."
- "Every tree that does not bear good fruit will be cut down and thrown into the fire."

Three points for Advent reflection at three levels of reflection: personal, national, and international. This is your challenge in this Advent season as you take seriously your responsibility to "prepare the way of the Lord."

3

Third Sunday of Advent

Isaiah 35:1–6a, 10; Psalm 146; James 5:7–10; Matthew 11:2–11

"BE PATIENT, BROTHERS AND SISTERS, UNTIL THE COMING OF THE LORD"

Advent is a good time to consider (or reconsider) the great Christian virtue of patience. The selection from the Letter of James that you heard in today's second reading puts it to you directly: "Be patient, brothers and sisters, until the coming of the Lord." And you might find yourself saying, "Yeah, right; but patience has never been my strong suit." If that, in fact, is the way it is with you—if patience is not your strong suit—then stay with the Letter of James for a few more reflective moments.

After urging you to be patient, James continues: "See how the farmer waits for the precious fruit of the earth, being patient with it until it receives the early and the late rains. You too must be patient."

"You too," James might have said, "must be obedient to the laws of growth." Think about that. Be obedient to the laws of growth. The farmer waits. The farmer cannot force the plant to grow. The farmer can nurture, till the soil around the plant, irrigate, fertilize; but the farmer cannot force the plant to grow. Nor can you, even if you tried, break the speed limits on the road to growth—to maturity, to healing or recovery of health, to mastery of ideas, languages, or developing human relationships. It all takes time. It takes a lot of patience.

Advent puts you in a spiritual state of expectancy—a spiritual state. Some years ago on the First Sunday of Advent, the late and beloved Fr. John Ciani stood in this pulpit here at Holy Trinity, spread out his arms to give the purple vestments full display, and then proclaimed to the amusement (and amazement) of all: "I'm expecting a baby!"

All of us are expecting. Advent puts us in a spiritual state of expectancy. Advent expectancy provides us with an opportunity to think about the virtue of patience in our lives.

The Letter of James continues: "Make your hearts firm, because the coming of the Lord is at hand. Do not complain, brothers and sisters, about one another, that you may not be judged." (James might just as easily and correctly have said, "Don't grow impatient with one another.") "Take as an example of hardship and patience, brothers and sisters, the prophets who spoke in the name of the Lord."

Then the Gospel reading gives you John the Baptist. Somehow or other, I have the feeling that patience, as we usually think about it, was not the strong suit of John the Baptist either. He was forceful, strong, even impulsive in a holy way. An admirable man, as we all acknowledge, but probably not a model of patience—even though his was a ministry of preparation for the coming of the Lord—faithful preparation, a ministry of faith-based patience. We participate in that mission of preparing the way of the Lord, the coming of the Lord once again into our world, into our midst, in our times. There can indeed by a coming of the presence of the Lord through our smiles, our words, our kindnesses, our deeds—great and small. So, if we are to meet our preparation responsibilities at all adequately, we have to come to terms with our difficulties with patience in daily life, with our impulse toward impatience in the practice of life.

What is patience? Dictionaries tell you it is about bearing pains or trials without complaint. It is showing forbearance under stress. It has something to do with being steadfast. Some would say that patience is "calm acceptance of whatever the Lord allows in my life today." It can also be said that patience is learning to put up with yourself.

I went on the Internet and found the following four "deft definitions of patience": (1) It is the art of losing temper very slowly; (2) It is the art of concealing impatience; (3) It is something while driving, that you appreciate in the drivers behind you, and resent in the one ahead of you; (4) It is the art of waiting for those who come late.

However you define or describe patience, you know that it exacts a price. Either way you pay. You pay in the coin of self-restraint in order to practice patience. You pay in the coin of regret if you fail to be patient. Your better self is diminished by impatience; your true self in enlarged through the practice of patience.

Look at the word etymologically. It is related to passion, and passion means to suffer. Recall the passion of Christ—the passion and death of Jesus.

Action and passion: The agent acts on a patient; the patient suffers (receives) the action. Patience literally means suffering. The agent acts; the patient receives the action. How a person receives the action—especially an unwanted action—is the test of patience. Tests of patience can come from countless sources: a dentist's drill, a honking horn, a fist pounding on the table, a spoken contradiction, an unmerited rebuke. The question is: How do you respond? And that, of course, is the test of patience.

Patience may not be your strong suit, but patience is part of the human condition. Or, to put it another way, patience makes the human condition bearable.

Although not included in today's readings, St. Paul's words speak to you today just as surely as they spoke to the Colossians (3:12–15) centuries ago: "Put on then, as God's chosen ones, holy and beloved, heartfelt compassion, kindness, humility, gentleness, and patience, bearing with one another and forgiving one another, if one has a grievance against another; as the Lord has forgiven you, so must you also do. And over all these put on love."

Think of patience as part of your wardrobe—there it is on the rack, in your closet, along with compassion, kindness, humility, and gentleness. Dress yourself in this kind of clothing. "And over all these put on love."

They never go out of style—these wraps, this wardrobe. As the liturgy today suggests, the recommended Advent fashion is patience. Put it on. Wrap yourself in it. Use it as a protection against the darts, daggers, itches, obstacles, frustrations, and irritations that are part of life all year round.

Just so that you will not become discouraged, let me suggest that from your impatience and its familiar causes in your own experience, realize that you can learn, you can profit, you can grow. You can, if you learn obedience to the laws of growth, become patient with yourself.

You can grow in the direction of patient compassion toward others, precisely because you have first suffered, and it is out of your sufferings—great or small—that patience will emerge.

"Be patient, brothers and sisters, until the coming of the Lord." Remember, my friends, that no matter how you cut it, patience will exact some toll in the form of suffering. That's the meaning of the word *suffer*. You cannot escape it. You may not grow to like it, but I can assure you, your patience will enable you to grow.

4

Fourth Sunday of Advent

Isaiah 7:10–14; Psalm 24; Romans 1:1–7; Matthew 1:18–24

BETWEEN LAW AND LOVE

The Gospel reading on this Fourth Sunday of Advent brings you directly into the Christmas mystery as it puts the spotlight on the great St. Joseph, the just man, who was betrothed to Mary. When you meet Joseph in this story from the opening chapter in the Gospel of Matthew, he and Mary had not yet lived together but, as the Scripture story tells you, "she was found to be with child through the Holy Spirit." Joseph, when you meet him here, is on the line, so to speak. I like to identify it as the line between law and love.

The law says that Mary had to be set aside, cut off, divorced; she was unmarried but "with child." She was engaged to Joseph, but according to the law, that engagement must now be broken. Love prompted Joseph to want to spare her any pain and publicity. An even deeper love prompted him to take God's message and messenger seriously. "Joseph, son of David," said the angel who appeared to him in a dream, "do not be afraid to take Mary your wife into your home. For it is through the Holy Spirit that this child has been conceived in her." Joseph decided to trust God, to break the law, and to set up a household with Mary, even though he could not unravel the mystery surrounding her.

Try to imagine the fix Joseph found himself to be in—right there on the line between law and love. You will find yourself on that same line from time to time on your journey through life, right there on the line between law and love. As you traverse that line, you will find, as Joseph did, that there is only one absolute and that one absolute is the will of

God. You will also find that there is only one ultimate law for you, and that's the law of love.

This is not to say that you should have no respect for human law. It is simply to say that you are capable of using the law as a substitute for responsible decision making, as a shield against growth-producing choice. You can substitute external authority for internal integrity. You can permit the letter of the law to stifle the life-giving potential of courageous love. Or you can follow the promptings of your heart and face up to the legal consequences of what might be perceived by others as an illegal action. All the while you can work to change the law to let it embody more fully the principles of love. That's how Joseph became a saint!

Now it is true that God's will in all of this was disclosed to Joseph is an unusual way. God's messenger—the angel—appeared to him in a dream. That is not likely to happen to you or me. We've got to be attentive to our feelings—how we feel about the alternative paths that we might take, how we feel about the options before us, where we feel God is calling us, what we think and feel God is asking us to do, to be, to become. This is what the spiritual writers call discernment, discernment of spirits.

Faith tells us that there are good and evil spirits at work in our world. The "push" or "pull" within you can be from God or not from God. You have to discern the origin of a particular "movement" or feeling within. In order to do that, you have to locate yourself, you have to give yourself a fair reading of where you stand before God. Are you moving away from God—on a downward slope; or are you trying to let yourself be drawn toward God—moving in the right direction? Beware of anxiety and discouragement when you are doing your best to move toward God; they come from the evil spirit. Heed the pangs of conscience when you are on the down side; the good spirit is trying to get through to you.

You have many decisions to make as you move through life. God is not a disinterested observer. God is calling you, prompting you; in a very real sense of the word, God is rooting for you. You've got to figure out the direction in which God is calling you to move, just as Joseph had to figure things out.

If you are going to decide well, you have to first discern well; and the target of your discernment is the will of God for you. Locating yourself in prayer before God means that you are self-aware. You will also be sufficiently quiet, as Joseph was, to detect the movements of competing spirits.

The Lord will give you a sign, as he gave a sign to Joseph. You can count on it. But if you want that to happen, you have to take care now to be like Joseph, a just person, a good person, a generous person, a loving person whose heart was open to whatever God willed for him.

Once you decide there on the line between law and love, you will know that your decision is the right one when you experience peace of heart, a confirmatory tranquility, a deep and abiding joy. If the opposite is there—turmoil, anxiety—reopen the discernment process and continue your search for the will of God.

Whatever you find yourself doing in life, whatever your occupation may be, you will find that you have to live your life between law and love, drawing on both, permitting one to discipline the other. You will lean from time to time more toward one than toward the other, but for the sake of your personal happiness and the good of the world around you, you can never allow the love in your heart to be crushed by the weight of legalism. What if Joseph had done what the law required, once he learned that Mary was with child?

II
Christmas

. . . .

5

Christmas Vigil

Isaiah 62:1–5; Psalm 89; Acts 13:16–17, 22–25; Matthew 1:1–25

WE ARE ALL MEANT TO BE MOTHERS OF GOD

Eckhart von Hochheim, the German Dominican and early fourteenth-century writer of mystical theology, is better known as Meister Eckhart. "Meister" is a German word that simply means master—a master teacher. He once said: "What good is it to me if Mary gave birth to the son of God and I do not also give birth to the son of God in my own time and my own culture? We are all meant to be Mothers of God for God is always needing to be born."

Think about that. An interesting idea. God is always needing to be born. But how? How can Jesus be born again? Meister Eckhart is suggesting that Jesus can be brought to life again by you and me.

Each one of you is called to be the Mother of God—the mother of Jesus. How can that be? Well, it has to be because God wants to be born again in our world, wherever there's need today for love, for peace, for healing, for instruction, for shelter, for nutrition, for redemption, for joy, for all those gifts that Jesus brought with him into the life of the human family. Through his birth in human form, he became good news to the world. God wants to be born again in our day so that this good news, these good things, can become visible in our midst.

But, you might say, "I'm a boy; I'm twelve years old. How can I be the Mother of God?" Well, you might meet other boys in the school-yard or playground—boys and girls too—who need a friend; who need protection from bullies; who need a word of encouragement, a helping hand. You can be the heart and hand of Jesus reaching out to them. You can bring Christ to birth in the midst of human need that twelve-year-olds know and feel.

19

"But I'm a grandmother," you might say, "how can I be the Mother of God?" Well you might meet younger mothers who need help with their young families. You may be aware of sick or lonely people who need company. You can bring Christ into their lives—with a visit, with a card, with an offer to sit in for a few hours to give young mothers a break.

"But I'm in mid-career," you might say. "I'm a man or woman fully engaged in business or the professions; how can I be the Mother of God?" Well, Christ surely wants to come to birth in the marketplace, in the world of ideas, in the public square. The Prince of Peace needs to appear once more in the midst of violence, loneliness, contentions, and disputes. The sun of justice wants to rise again in the midst of injustice and misunderstanding. You can make that happen.

"I'm chronically ill; I can't do anything," you might be thinking. "How can I bring Christ to birth?" Your limitations, your pain, your discouragement, your loneliness can have redemptive power. You can unite all that with the sufferings of Christ for the salvation of the world.

"I'm a high school senior. I'm not yet ready. Besides, I've got to worry about getting into college and making new friends and getting along better with the friends I already have." No, you have time. Just think of it as taking time to be considerate, thoughtful, respectful of others your age and older. Take time out from the rush to consider how much you have to be grateful for and then give thanks to God by being good to the children of God you meet around you.

"What good is it to me if Mary gave birth to the Son of God and I do not also give birth to the Son of God in my own time and my own culture? We are all meant to be Mothers of God, for God is always needing to be born." There's a lot of wisdom in those words. There's a lot for each one of us here to think about. There's a lot of Christmas to be made if we decide to get to work and start making it right here, right now.

This doesn't man running out and buying gifts. This means resolving to make a gift of yourself to others. That's the Christmas spirit; and you can bring it to birth in your own family, neighborhood, school, work-place. You can be joy to the world!

Another mystic, it may have been Teresa of Avila, has written:

Christ has no body now but yours,
No hands, no feet on earth but yours,
Yours are the eyes with which he looks with
compassion on this world,
Yours are the feet with which he walks about doing good,
Yours are the hands, with which he blesses all the world.

Think about that as we celebrate the birth of Christ on this Christmas Vigil. Today, your hands are his hands, your feet are his feet, your eyes his eyes. Just by willing it, you can bring him to birth in your world!

"What good is it to [you] if Mary gave birth to the son of God and [you] do not also give birth to the son of God in [your] own time and [your] own culture?

"We are all meant to be Mothers of God for God is always needing to be born."

A merry and blessed Christmas to you all, and, through you, may abundant blessings and abiding peace come to the corner of the world that you call home.

6

Christmas Mass at Midnight

Isaiah 9:1–6; Psalm 96; Titus 2:11–14; Luke 2:1–14

COUNTING YOUR BLESSINGS

"You have nothing to fear! I come to proclaim good news to you—tidings of great joy to be shared by the whole people." That's what the angel said, and you know what those tidings of great joy were. So let's reflect on the good news, let's run a check on the level of joy in our lives right now.

There is no way of measuring the discontent that lies hidden beneath the lights and festive happenings of Christmas and Hanukkah in America this year. No need to try. But it is worth reflecting for a moment or two this evening on the fact that Christmas is not automatically merry for all Christians, and that the holidays are not necessarily happy for everyone.

Wishing will not change that, but facing up to reality can.

Part of the attitudinal realignment that reality can provide is recognition of the fact that it is impossible to be simultaneously grateful and unhappy. Let me repeat that: It is impossible for anyone to be simultaneously grateful and unhappy. So, if you are even a little bit unhappy on this Christmas Eve, you should run a gratitude check on yourself. Counting your blessings and giving thanks for them is a surefire way of closing the happiness deficit. We all have something to be grateful for; hence, none of us has an overpowering reason to be unhappy.

Similarly, recognition of the undeniable fact in human experience—yours and mine—that more is often not enough, can lower your expectations to a point that puts discontent in proper perspective. It is not just unrealistic, but silly, always to want more. This is the season to recognize that more is very often not enough. Sometimes less can be more as many

22

of the elders here tonight will acknowledge when they think of days gone by when they had less, were even perhaps poor, but they were happy.

This Christmas night is also the time to consider how to achieve more of whatever it is that might be called really important in life.

That thought came home to me recently as I read Philip Dray's book *There is Power in a Union: The Epic Story of Labor in America* (Doubleday). I had always thought labor leader Samuel Gompers gave a monosyllabic (and dollar-focused) reply in 1893 to the question, "What does labor want?" and that response was "More." But Philip Dray corrects my false impression by putting Gompers' complete reply on the record. To the question "What does labor want?" Gompers replied, "It wants the earth and the fullness thereof.... Labor wants more schoolhouses and less jail cells; more books and less arsenals; more learning and less vice; more leisure and less greed; more justice and less revenge; in fact, more of the opportunities to cultivate our better natures, and to make mankind more noble, womanhood more beautiful, and childhood more happy and bright."

The point Gompers wanted to make well over a century ago was that there is a whole range of reality beyond the paycheck, beyond money, beyond any material gift, there is a range of reality that needs enlargement and expansion in order to bring the good life within reach of ordinary people. His list of "wants" can serve us well as a catalog of blessings that deserve to be counted at this time of the year.

Take a moment tonight to count your blessing from "the earth and the fullness thereof"—the crops, the fruits and vegetables, the beauties of nature. Think of the schoolhouses, the books, learning and leisure; think of justice in our world, and the opportunities that are ours to make our lives more noble, beautiful, happy, and bright.

Take a moment tonight to give thanks for the gift of life, faith, and family, for good health, even when health may be slipping away in the late evening of life and the promise of eternal life may be an immediate reality. Think of the home and happiness, and loves that are yours every day, and give thanks for all of that. Giving thanks is a great way of opening the door to more joy, genuine joy, in your life.

As you know, things have been tough economically for many in our country in recent years. As you may also know, for each of the eleven months leading up to this Christmas 2010, the United States has seen a growth in new jobs, but at a rate insufficient to fuel a robust recovery from the Great Recession that began in 2008. This is a case of more jobs surely being not enough; many more will be needed in the years ahead. Let's pray for the unemployed tonight; let's think of what we might do to help them. Think of how a good job can bring joy into a human life.

More attention needs to be paid during the coming years to the nation's fiscal deficit, and more sacrifice in and out of government will be needed to correct it. You've read about that in the newspapers and heard about it on the radio and TV news. You may not understand it all, but you can be grateful if it has not affected you adversely; you can also be grateful for the opportunity that might be yours to contribute in some small way to the reduction of these great problems that surround us.

"More justice and less revenge," as Gompers put it, would be a welcome development in our world. Justice will surely be served by any effort to shift the burden of economic hardship from the unemployed and those who are foreclosed homeowners, to shift a small measure of that burden to the rest of us whose shared sacrifice could mean greater economic security for all.

More justice would be a great gift to our world and a blessing on families, cities, and beyond in a society where grateful people work for justice for all.

Christmas is a reminder that none of us has any good reason to be unhappy. We are blessed. We are redeemed—but we can also become forgetful. And the first sign of that forgetfulness is a twinge of unhappiness that may seep into your awareness when you notice that someone else has received more than you received this Christmas, that someone else has more of what you would like to have. That's the kind of "more" that will never be enough for you. Keep your eye and your heart fixed on the many good gifts that are already yours. Be grateful for them and be happy. "You have nothing to fear! I come to proclaim good news to you—tidings of great joy to be shared by the whole people."

Let that joy fill your hearts tonight. Merry Christmas!

7

Christmas Mass at Dawn

Isaiah 62:11–12; Psalm 97; Titus 3:4–7; Luke 2:15–20

WHEN THE KINDNESS AND LOVE OF GOD OUR SAVIOR APPEARED

The Church is inviting you, as dawn breaks over this Christmas morning, to reflect on the fact that "the kindness and love of God our savior appeared" on that first Christmas. That's how the Letter of Paul to Titus, your second reading in this morning's Mass, describes it.

You think of him who appeared as an infant, a beautiful newborn child. You also see with the eye of your imagination a manger, a stable, perhaps, or a cave. You think of Mary and Joseph, and shepherds standing by. You imagine it to be a silent night and acknowledge that it is indeed a holy night. You may think of it as chilly, a bit of snow perhaps. The eye of your imagination sees animals and straw. Above and beyond all this, the Church wants you to see something more—kindness and love—kindness and love incarnate, enfleshed; kindness and love as the original Christmas gift.

Kindness and love are immaterial realities. They cannot be seen, as such, just experienced. They cannot be weighed or measured, but they can be known just as you know with full certainty at this hour that God has delivered on his promise and sent his only Son to redeem you, to buy you back, to save you from your sins.

You were lost but now are found. You were dead, but now you live. And the Church is drawing on words from the Letter to Titus to put across to you a profound but simple point, namely, that because of Christmas, the kindness and love of God have a flesh-and-blood presence in your world, in your life, in your very self, in your very own day.

25

Now you might be saying to yourself, I can see kindness and love in Mary. I can see kindness and love in Joseph, but in this infant, in this speechless bundle of helpless dependency? All I can see there is need. All I can hear there is need. All I can touch there is need.

In much the same way that John Ciardi chose many years ago to title a book on poetry *How Does a Poem Mean?* the Church is inviting you into a mode of waiting watchfulness to learn over your lifetime and the lessons to be taught by this newborn Christ Child, "How do kindness and love enflesh themselves in our lives?"

Well, you must first understand that they enflesh themselves in persons, just as the second person of the Holy Trinity chose to do when he became man thus enfleshed—incarnate, as we say—kindness and love become visible to others, imitable by others, and eventually they will lead through the door of sacrifice to the salvation of others. That's the way it worked out in the life of Christ in whom kindness and love appeared and through whom kindness and love worked the salvation of the world.

The Church would make contemplatives of us all early on this Christmas morning. Look at the infant and contemplate kindness. Look at this holy Child and see the seeds of sacrifice. Look through this baby and see developing over the years—thirty-three of them—a man, true man, who is also true God before whom we, grateful mortals, bow at this moment in quiet adoration.

8

Christmas Mass during the Day

Isaiah 52:7–10; Psalm 98; Hebrews 1:1–6; John 1:1–18

BEHIND THE CHRISTMAS EVENT

Christmas peace! May abundant Christmas grace and joy be yours this morning.

The readings that the Church offers for your reflection in this third of our Christmas Masses celebrating the Nativity of the Lord, the readings of this "Mass During the Day," as it is called, are beautifully theological—mystical really—somewhat above or removed from the flesh-and-blood, straw-and-animal, manger-and-child, Madonna-and-Child picture that you carry in your imagination: the picture of Mary, Joseph and the Child, in a stable, surrounded by shepherds, as it is represented here at church in our Christmas crib. The message in this morning's readings invites you to close your eyes and move, as it were, through the proscenium of this manger scene to contemplate the reality of the awesome power of God that hovers above it all.

Reflect for a moment on the power of God at work in this event. Separate the event for a moment, if you can, from the mystery behind it and above it, in order to grasp, however incompletely, some understanding of God's eternal word, some measure of God's powerful love that lies hidden behind the Christmas event.

Forgive me, if you must, for being theological in this homily; thank me, if you will, for not being sentimental in talking about Christmas. I certainly do not want to be academic in these comments, but I do want to help you move through the tangible trappings to an appreciation and better understanding of the triumph of faith that awaits you in the contemplation of the scene of our Lord's Nativity.

Listen to one of the very early Church fathers, St. Hippolytus, who wrote many centuries ago: "God was all alone and nothing existed but himself when he determined to create the world. He thought of it, willed it, spoke the word and so made it....Apart from God there was simply nothing else. Yet although he was alone, he was manifold because he lacked neither reason, wisdom, power, nor counsel. All things were in him and he himself was all. At a moment of his own choosing and in a manner determined by himself, God manifested his Word (note that theologians explain this word to be not simply an external utterance, but the efficacious self-communication of God to the world; the word contains the power and dynamism of God's creative function) and through him [the Word] he made the whole universe."

Hippolytus continues: "When the Word was hidden within God himself, he was invisible to the created world, but God made him visible. First God gave utterance to his voice, engendering light from light, and then he sent his own mind into the world as its Lord. Visible before to God alone and not to the world, God made him visible so that the world could be saved by seeing him. This mind that entered our world was made known as the Son of God. All things came into being through him; but he alone is begotten by the Father." Beautiful. Profound. Worthy of reflection.

We bow before the manger in order that our mind's eye might move through the scene to behold the saving power that hovers over it. "God sent his own mind into the world" in this Christmas event!

Remember that as you ponder the words you just heard in the Gospel reading. They are familiar words from the prologue to the Gospel of John: "In the beginning was the Word, and the Word was with God, and the Word was God. He was in the beginning with God. All things came to be through him, and without him nothing came to be. What came to be through him was life, and this life was the light of the human race; the light shines in the darkness, and the darkness has not overcome it."

Nor, you can safely say, will the darkness of evil and sin, of terrorism and war, of hatred and injustice ever overcome it. Nor will the darkness of doubt that some of us have to deal with, nor the illnesses we bear, nor the reversals and disappointments that tend to get us down ever overcome us, so long as we turn to and remain close to the Light of the World.

"The true light," writes St. John in the words you heard proclaimed today, "The true light, which enlightens everyone, was coming into the world." That's what we see in this manger scene. "He was in the world, and the world came to be through him, but the world did not know him. He came to what was his own, but his own people did not accept him. But to those who did accept him (and that, dear friends, is a reference to every one of you!) he gave power to become children of God, to those who believe in his name (another reference to you!) who were born not by natural generation nor by human choice not by a man's decision but of God (a reference to your rebirth in baptism!)."

And then John gives the pronouncement that brings us to our knees in grateful adoration: "And the Word became flesh and made his dwelling among us, and we saw his glory, the glory as of the Father's only Son, full of grace and truth."

There is so much there to contemplate. There is so much cause for wonder. There is so much reason to be grateful. And there is so much hope waiting to work its way deeper into your heart, if only you will let the key of faith open your heart to receive it. No matter how bad things appear to be around you, no matter how little faith you have in yourself, no matter how frightened you are, no matter how guilty you feel, no matter how empty you may be today, fall on your knees before the mystery and majesty of Christmas and let this Infant do for you what he was born to do for all, namely, rescue you from the darkness, bring you into the light, save you from your sins, and offer you the promise of eternal life. Merry Christmas!

9

Feast of the Holy Family,
Sunday in the Octave of Christmas

Sirach 3:2–7, 12–14; Psalm 128; Colossians 3:12–21;
Matthew 2:13–15, 19–23

FORGIVENESS AND FAMILY HEALING

It is more than helpful from time to time simply to ponder in quiet prayer the depths of a few of the beautiful passages from Scripture that find their way into the wedding ceremony. One that I particularly like is the selection from Paul's Letter to the Colossians that you heard today as the second reading on this Holy Family Sunday:

> Put on then, as God's chosen ones, holy and beloved,
> heartfelt compassion, kindness, humility, gentleness, and
>   patience,
> bearing with one another and forgiving one another,
> if anyone has a complaint against another;
> as the Lord has forgiven you, so must you also do.
> And over all these put on love,
> that is, the bond of perfection.
> And let the peace of Christ control your hearts,
> the peace into which you were also called into one body.
> And be thankful.

This text emerged in separate contexts, several years apart, in a way that touched profoundly the lives of two couples—one whose marriage had reached the breaking point, the other whose marriage had just begun. Let me explain; and as I do, consider the power of forgiveness in family healing.

It was a bit of a risk, I knew, to inject a sad, although beautiful, story into the homily I gave at Holy Trinity Parish in Georgetown, during my final wedding as pastor there in the summer of 2003. The bride and groom, Trisha Morrow and Matt Madden, had selected this passage from Colossians as the second reading for their wedding liturgy. Shortly before the ceremony took place, I received a letter that reminded me that I had preached on that same text from Colossians at a Sunday Mass several years before. I took the risk of quoting from this moving and quite personal communication in my words to Matt and Trish.

The letter was from a woman I do not know, a parishioner who wrote to wish me well as I was leaving Holy Trinity and to tell me a story of how, without knowing it, I had touched her life. She explained that she and her husband were married at Trinity in 1974. "Like most long unions," she wrote, "we encountered a rocky period in our marriage, leading to a separation in July of 2000. In December of 2000, New Year's Eve, he approached me about reconciliation."

She said that she reacted to that proposal with "pain and anger," but "I was also very undecided." Her letter went on to say that on the next Sunday, which would have been Holy Family Sunday, "I attended Mass where you gave a sermon on forgiveness. You gave me much to think about." Shortly thereafter, she said, she began meeting with her husband to begin "talking and exploring our mistakes....Forgiveness is not an easy, instant accomplishment, and I owe you a great appreciation for opening my eyes to that."

Her letter went on to relate that "in the summer of 2002, we traveled to Ireland to celebrate my fiftieth birthday. Unbeknownst to me, he had arranged with the parish priest for us to renew our vows at the Catholic church in Kinsdale, County Cork. It became the highlight of our trip and an opportunity for us to renew our devotion to each other with Christ's blessing."

The writer added that two months later her husband died in a cycling accident. "Although our reconciliation was short, I am indebted to you for teaching me the importance of forgiveness and love in my life."

As I mentioned, Trish and Matt had selected Colossians 3:12–17 for their second reading. "Put on then, as God's chosen ones, holy and beloved, heartfelt compassion, kindness, humility, gentleness, and patience, bearing with one another and forgiving one another, if one has a grievance against another; as the Lord has forgiven you, so must you also do."

When I realized that this reading was the one my correspondent had heard on the Holy Family Sunday she referenced in her letter, I decided to share the story with Matt and Trish and their wedding guests. In my words at their wedding, I reminded Matt and Trish that love and forgiveness are one. The Letter to the Colossians lists love's central elements. It explains the meaning of love in terms that constitute a charter for a happy marriage. I held in my hand a copy of that Holy Family Sunday homily of three years before, and from it I read my own words:

Aware of having been forgiven and yet still needing forgiveness in Jesus Christ, believers should extend to each other forgiveness now and the promise of future forgiveness. That, of course, is what it means to forgive as the Lord had forgiven you.

And I added these additional words from the Letter to the Colossians: "And over all these put on love, that is, the bond of perfection. And let the peace of Christ control your hearts, the peace into which you were also called in one body. And be thankful."

These are potent words for newlyweds as well as for those who are hopeful of staying wed when "a rocky period" threatens their marriage.

I write a biweekly syndicated column for the Catholic News Service. It is a general interest column that allows me a wide enough range of topics to include occasional thoughts about marriage and the family. So I wrote a column about the story I've just related here; it appeared in many diocesan newspapers around the country under the title, "When a Rocky Period Threatens a Marriage." To my surprise, it prompted the following letter from Matt Madden:

Trish and I recently received a copy of your September 19th column that ran in the [Boston] *Pilot,* in which you reference the homily you delivered at our wedding in July. We appreciated your thoughtful words on love and forgiveness at our wedding and are very happy you were able to share this message with a wider audience.

We are glad you took "a bit of a risk" to tell a story that demonstrated the importance of forgiveness in marriage. The words you spoke, as well as those in the Holy Family Sunday homily you gave us afterward, will certainly be an important part of our lives together as we work to deepen our vocation to celebrate and bear witness to Christ's love as a couple.

What you may not have known is what a particular blessing this "risk" was at our ceremony. Trish's parents, only a year and a half before our wedding, had separated and moved apart. Their struggles as a couple were difficult for them as well as for Trish and me. For a year and a half they took slow but deliberate steps toward reconciliation and forgiveness. Just a few months before our wedding they resumed living under the same roof to continue their process of reuniting and resuming their lives together. Their progress continues and it is wonderful to witness this power of forgiveness that you spoke of in your homily.

I believe that our wedding preparations were an important part of Mr. and Mrs. Morrow's reconciliation as much as watching their work toward forgiveness was an important part of our spiritual preparation for marriage. Issues of reconciliation, forgiveness, marital strife, and what it means to be a Christian couple pervaded many of my conversations with Trish as we prepared for our wedding. Therefore, it was a special blessing that you chose this theme for your homily on our wedding day....

Thank you for being an important part of our important day. You couldn't have chosen a better message to guide Trish and me, as well as our friends and family, on the day of our wedding. It was a special gift of the Holy Spirit that you were called to take this "risk" at our wedding and a gift for which we are extremely grateful.

Well there's a Holy Family homily for you in letter form. It is also an example of how nice it is to be remembered and reminded, from time to time, about the power of forgiveness in family healing.

10

January 1, Octave of Christmas, Solemnity of Mary, Mother of God

Numbers 6:22–27; Psalm 67; Galatians 4:4–7; Luke 2:16–21

"AND MARY KEPT ALL THESE THINGS, REFLECTING ON THEM IN HER HEART" (LUKE 2:19)

Catholics are asking a lot of questions about Mary these days. For instance, a good Catholic woman well into her seventies said to me a few years ago, "I find it awkward to raise the question but I find myself wondering about Mary. I know she's special. I believe that she's the Mother of God. But why is it that there seems always to have been more interest in Mary among Catholics than non-Catholic Christians, and why is it that in recent years Catholics seem to be toning down their devotion to the Blessed Mother?"

Well, that's a good question and it happened to be Christmastime when she asked it, a very good time to raise a question about Mary, whose likeness appears in Christmas art and Christmas cards as well as the familiar Christmas crèche or crib. Two phrases from a most familiar prayer can help to get a response to that question going: "Ave Maria" and "Sancta Maria."

When you pray, "Hail," "Hello," or "Ave" Maria, you are recalling a moment beautifully depicted by Henry Ossawa Tanner (1859–1937) in an oil-on-canvas painting entitled "The Annunciation" (1898), which hangs in the Philadelphia Museum of Art. (Your Internet search engine can find the image for you.) In the picture, Mary is an ordinary girl, a dark-haired adolescent dressed in rumpled Middle Eastern peasant clothing. The angel Gabriel is depicted as a shaft of light in the corner of the room. His message, of course, is the startling announcement that Mary is to be the Mother of God. Every "Hail Mary," every "Ave Maria" recalls that announcement, which, because it was directed solely to the teenaged Mary, made her truly unique.

"Sancta Maria," that words that open the second half of that familiar prayer, affirm not only that Mary was the "Mater Dei," but also that she was holy—so much so that her prayers for us "now and at the hour of our death" are uniquely powerful before God.

The Church has solemnly declared Mary to have been free of original sin from the first moment of her existence. It proclaims her to have given Jesus life "by the power of the Holy Spirit," and to have experienced just a "blink" of death followed by a bodily assumption into heaven.

Catholic devotion over the centuries has tended to focus on and celebrate the "in-imitable" virtues of Mary—her immaculate conception, virgin birth, divine maternity, assumption, her status as Queen of Heaven—so much so that some otherwise devout Catholics regard her as out of reach when, in fact, her greatest virtue was her faith, a clearly imitable quality exhibited by her response to Gabriel when she was a teenager: "Be it done unto me according to your word" (Luke 1:38). Mary hears the word of God and acts upon it. She is thus a disciple who commits herself to an uncertain future. I like to think of her as "Our Lady of Faith."

Because devotion to Mary was so prominent and intense in Catholic circles in decades past, non-Catholic Christians often chose to separate themselves a bit from Marian devotional practices in order to establish their denominational apartness. Moreover, those who were hostile or just unfriendly to the Church years ago were put off by what they saw as excess in Marian devotion. They accused Catholics of practicing "Mariolatry."

But some first-rate Protestant scholars are now in serious dialogue with Catholic scholars about Mary; the ecumenical gap, relative to Mary, is narrowing.

Among Catholics, Mary's appeal is reemerging. It is nice to be able to celebrate that on this first day of the New Year, this "Solemnity of Mary, the Mother of God."

There is a lovely poem about Mary, written centuries ago by Boccachio, that contains words I've often pondered on the Feast of Mary's Assumption. It also offers a word picture of Mary—part of which, a reference to her "braids of gold" and "queenly dress"—would conflict with the dark-skinned, dark-haired, simply garbed teenager in Henry Tanner's painting. And I would judge Tanner's painting to offer a more authentic representation. In any case, think of Mary as you listen to these words:

> Not braids of gold, nor beauty in thy eyes,
> Nor queenly dress, nor winsome maiden grace,
> Nor youthfulness, nor music's melodies,
> Nor loveliness of angel in thy face,
> Could draw the king of heaven from sovereign place
> To this our life of guilt and sordidness
> To be made flesh in thee, Mary, Mother of grace,
> Mirror of joy and all our happiness,
>
> But thy humility—so great in thee,
> It broke the ancient barrier of wrath
> Twixt God and us, to open heaven's bars.
> Then of thy virtue lend to us that we,
> May follow, Holy Mother, in thy path
> Unwavering, to rise beyond the stars.

As I say, I love those beautiful words and meditate on them on the Feast of the Assumption, the day of Mary's bodily arrival into heaven— she was "assumed" into heaven, we say, and that doctrine was defined—that is, proposed infallibly for belief by all Catholics—by Pope Pius XII in 1950.

As I've indicated, I think we fail to appreciate as fully as we should the fact that Mary was a woman of faith. Faith, in my view, was her great virtue—one, by the way, that is clearly imitable by all of us. Because she believed, she was prompt and unhesitating in following God's will for her. She was and surely is our Queen Mother. And we honor her in that capacity today. But she was also a woman of faith, and we resolve today to imitate her in the practice of that great virtue.

Listen to the great St. Augustine extolling Our Lady's faith. First he refers to the Gospel of Matthew (12:46–50) where you will read: "Stretching out his hand over his disciples, the Lord Christ declared: 'Here are my mother and my brothers, anyone who does the will of my Father who sent me is my brother and my sister and my mother.'" This, you may remember, was said in reply to someone who asked Jesus who his mother was. And he says, in effect, those who believe and do my Father's will are mother, brother, sister to me. In any case, St. Augustine continues in his homiletic reflection on this incident with these words: "Did the Virgin Mary, who believed by faith and conceived by faith, who was the chosen one from whom our Savior was born among men, who was created by Christ before Christ was created in her—did she not do the will of the Father? Indeed blessed Mary certainly did the Father's will, and so it was for her a greater thing to have been Christ's disciple than to have been his mother, and she was more blessed in her discipleship than in her motherhood." There she is—our Lady of Faith.

And there she is, the woman we honor today, Mary, the Mother of God.

11

Second Sunday after Christmas

Sirach 24:1–4, 8–12; Psalm 147;
Ephesians 1:3–6, 15–18; John 1:1–18

IN THE BEGINNING

Let me suggest that you think about Christmas as a new beginning. It was a new beginning over two thousand years ago for the whole human race, to be sure, but think about it now as a new beginning for you, each one of you, in this Christmas season. It is Christmas. Think of it as something new, for you, this year.

The Fourth Gospel, the Gospel of St. John, opens with these words: "In the beginning…."

"In the beginning was the word." "*In principio erat verbum*" is the Latin version of that message that the elders among you will remember hearing in what was called the "Last Gospel" that was read at the end of every Mass before the liturgical changes that came after the Second Vatican Council.

> In the beginning was the Word,
> and the Word was with God,
> and the Word was God.
> He was in the beginning with God.
> All things came to be through him,
> and without him nothing came to be.
> What came to be through him was life,
> and this life was the light of the human race;
> the light shines in the darkness,
> and the darkness has not overcome it.

Reflect on what you just heard. The "Word," the "Verbum," refers to Jesus Christ, the Second Person of our Triune God—Father, Son, and Holy Spirit. The divine Word, spoken, as it were, by the Father, is the Christ of Christmas. He was there at the beginning—before time, from all eternity—but not as Christ, rather as the Word, the creating Word of God.

It was not until the first Christmas night, the silent night, the holy night, that the divine Word, who had taken human flesh by the Holy Spirit in the womb of the Virgin Mary nine months previously, was born as Christ our Lord. Listen to the continuation of the prologue of St. John's Gospel:

He was in the world,
and the world came to be through him,
but the world did not know him.
He came to what was his own [i.e., to us, to you and me, to the
    human race],
But his own people did not accept him.

But to those who did accept him
he gave power to become children of God,
to those who believe in his name,
who were born not of natural generation
nor by human choice nor by a man's decision
but of God.

In other words, John is saying, to those who, like you and me, have been born again by faith, power is given to become children of God. You and I are thus empowered; we are adopted sons and daughters of the Triune God. And we celebrate at Christmastime the birth of the One who made this happen, who brought this about, who created our world and recreated us.

St. John goes on to say in the concluding words of the prologue to his Gospel:

And the Word became flesh
and made his dwelling among us [the literal meaning of the
   Greek verb used by John is, "he pitched his tent among us"],
and we saw his glory,
the glory as of the Father's only Son,
full of grace and truth.

Those are truly remarkable as well as beautiful words. They are yours to ponder at this hour. Make them your own as you reflect on the meaning of Christmas as a new beginning this year for you.

I'd like to suggest three locations in your life, or three areas where a new beginning can take place right now. The first is *forgiveness*; the second is *family*: and the third is *giving*.

Forgiveness—when I mention that word, what comes immediately to your mind? Are you holding back right now, refusing to forgive someone, or refusing to forgive yourself? Or, are you too proud to ask another for forgiveness?

Consider how forgiveness and apology are first cousins; they live at opposite ends of the same street. Take a look at both ends of the street for a moment at Christmastime.

You may find it very hard to say, "I apologize," even when you know you should. Well, Christmas is the time to say that word. Whenever that word is spoken, it calls for a response in the vocabulary of forgiveness. Someone once said that "the singular achievement of [an apology] …resides in is capacity to effectively eradicate the consequences of the offense by evoking the unpredictable faculty of forgiveness." There's a very nice thought—wonderful, isn't it, how certain words at certain times can make a problem disappear?

Are you refusing to forgive, when someone else says to you "I'm sorry, I apologize"? Or has your own expression of sorrow, your apology, fallen on deaf ears, not drawn the hoped-for response of forgiveness? As I said, forgiveness and apology are opposite ends on the same street. Christmas may be the time for you to take a walk up and down that street, to figure out where you are in your relationship with someone you may have hurt, or who may have hurt you, or figure out where you are in your relationship with yourself perhaps, and simply decide to say in faith and humility—in the true Christmas spirit—whatever it is that must be said, so that you can take your proper place in the Christmas celebration.

Forgive, as the Lord has forgiven you. Forgiveness is the foundation of the Christmas mystery. It is the reason why the Son of God took our flesh, was born, and "pitched his tent among us"—forgiveness.

The second area for thinking about a new beginning in your life at Christmastime is family. This is a family celebration, a family feast. Just being together as a family is a source of strength and joy; or, at least, it should be. We acknowledge that Christmas carries an edge of sadness for those who lost a family member recently. Christmas can also see the rise of family tensions and pressures—that's why forgiveness is so important at this time of year.

But best of all, Christmas brings us back in touch with the Holy Family—Mary, Joseph and their infant Son—and just picturing them in the simple surroundings of the cave or stable in Bethlehem can serve to remind us moderns of the importance of simplicity in family life and love. There was nothing commercial about the first Christmas, nothing expensive, nothing stylish. There was just family love. And to the extent that we admit the expensive and the stylish, to the extent that the products of commerce find their way into our celebration of Christmas, we have to take great care that we do not permit ourselves to be possessed by our possessions, or obsessed with the material side of Christmas to the point of losing touch with the simplicity that makes it all so beautiful and full of meaning. That brings me to my third point, the third location in your life where the new beginning of Christmas can find its way into your life—generosity.

You've been generous to others and others have been generous to you in the Christmas gift exchange. But think for a moment about the meaning of generosity. Surely, it is not a form of bribery. You don't purchase affection with your gifts. Surely, generosity is not a mask for lording it over others, dominating them with the power of your purse. Generosity puts the other person first. It is a way of opening your heart to another. Generosity is one way you have of affirming another. Generosity is one way you have of imitating God. Generosity is an opportunity to be good just for the sake of being good.

You've heard it said that cleanliness is next to godliness, that to forgive is divine. Well consider how generosity can put you right up there with the Giver of all gifts, on a plane with the good and generous Creator of all we have. Your generosity can be your participation in divine creativity. Just let it happen. Just be generous. Let it be part of your new beginning in this Christmas season.

12

January 6, Epiphany

Isaiah 60:1–6; Psalm 72; Ephesians 3:2–3, 5–6;
Matthew 2:1–12

BREAKING THROUGH

The theme and spirit of Epiphany is struck by the opening words in today's first reading, the selection from the Prophet Isaiah: "Rise up in splendor, Jerusalem! Your light has come, the glory of the Lord shines upon you."

Think of yourselves as Jerusalem—not a place, but a people, a special group set apart. And hear the word of God addressed directly to you today encouraging you to "rise up," to stand up, to set yourselves apart, to show forth your difference to the rest of the world. And what is that difference? The fact that you are in possession of God-made-man, the God-man. You are in possession of the divine word, the Second Person of the Blessed Trinity, who has come to you, has taken possession of you, redeemed you, bought you back, saved you from your sins, won for you the gift of eternal life.

Epiphany is an invitation to let all this break through and out so that others can see—and themselves be touched by the wonder of it all. The very word *epiphany*—a combination of two Greek words: *epi*, a prefix meaning "bump up against, show forth"; and *phano*, a word familiar to you from the English "fantasy" and "fantastic" and all that is suggested by the "light shows" with which modern electronics have made you familiar—the word *epiphany* speaks to you of showing forth, breaking through, letting light shine forth.

So don't be passive today. This is Epiphany. This is time to look up and out, to shine forth, to witness to something quite literally spectacular and that, of course, is the presence in our midst of the Light of the World.

But close your eyes for a moment and think outside the walls of this church. Think your way across this city, in and out of homes. Think up and down the corridors of hospitals. Think of prisons and the dark corners of despair. Think of hunger, poverty, homelessness, and hopelessness. Now open your eyes again and look around you. What are you—all of you—going to do to brighten up your world? You can choose to be passive, but there is nothing of Epiphany in passivity. You can choose to be silent—not discuss any of this with others—but somehow or other silence and Epiphany seem to be incompatible. When light breaks out, when "the glory of the Lord" breaks forth, there has to be some expression of wonder, joy, gladness, gratitude, and there has to be a desire to share this good news. Epiphany propels all that!

It propels some understandable emotion. It should propel some kind of motion on your part. At the very least it can bring a smile to your face, a lilt to your voice. Your smile, your voice can witness to the presence of Christ in our world. You don't necessarily have to do anything extraordinary. You can simply smile. You can simply show forth kindness in view of the extraordinary kindness that has been shown to you.

The Epiphany story comes to us from Matthew's Gospel in the account of the three kings or "wise men"—"astrologers" in Matthew's description. They knew nothing about light shows but they did know something about the wisdom of reading the signs of the times and the importance of following their "lights," their vocational "stars" wherever God would have them go.

So you don't necessarily have to think today about changing the world. Just think of changing yourself. Change your direction if the "star" God wants you to follow is leading to something new. Be a witness, a cheerful, grateful witness to the appearance of God-made-man in our world.

And, in the spirit of the Magi, think about any gifts you might want to bring to your newborn king. Gold, frankincense, and myrrh were the gifts the Magi brought. Tradition sees gold as recognition of the kingship of Christ; incense suggests his divinity; and myrrh points to his eventual redemptive suffering. You can decide for yourself today how you want to align yourself with his kingship; relate to his divinity, and participate in his suffering. All I'm suggesting is that you wear a smile on your face today to show forth your absolute delight that the infant king has found a place in your heart.

13

Baptism of the Lord

Isaiah 42:1–4, 6–7; Psalm 29; Acts 10:34–38; Matthew 3:13–17

MY FAVOR RESTS ON HIM

There are words in today's Gospel reading that each of us needs to hear. I would even make bold to say that each of us *deserves* to hear these words. Not that we merit to hear them, but we deserve to hear them because God so chooses to have it that way. And, if the truth be told, you have to admit that it is difficult to make it through this present life without the conviction that these words convey. So accept them; make them your own prized possession.

The words I'm referring to are there in the Gospel of Matthew who portrays Jesus coming forth from Galilee and presenting himself at the Jordan River to John the Baptist to be baptized by him—to be inducted into the community of like-minded men and women whom John, whose mission was, as you will recall, "to prepare the way of the Lord," had formed. And, as Matthew relates it, after Jesus had emerged from the baptismal waters of the River Jordan, "the sky opened and he [Jesus] saw the Spirit of God descend like a dove and hover over him. With that, a voice from the heavens said, 'This is my beloved Son. My favor rests on him.'"

Those are the words God wants you to hear today; those are the words God wants you to apply to yourself: "This is my beloved son [or daughter]." And God wants you to understand that his "favor" rests on you. Favor is another word for grace. You are graced; you are favored. But you have to believe this—that you are indeed favored. You have to have the courage to take God at his word. This truth has to become a living part of you and only you can let that happen.

No false humility now—no looking left and right and saying, in effect, "OK, they apply to him or her, but not to me." Yes, they do apply to you. That is the point of this baptismal renewal Jesus wants you to experience today as you recall his baptism by John there at the Jordan River.

He wants you to look up, as he looked up, and to see the heavens open and the Holy Spirit come down upon you like a gentle dove; and with that descent come the words of God: "This is my beloved son, [my beloved daughter] upon whom my favor rests."

Put it this way: you are favored. You are one of God's favorites. And just because God has many favorites, that is no reason at all for you to conclude that you are not special. God is, after all, God. And your all-powerful God can have as many favorites as he desires. Rejoice in the knowledge that you are one of them.

I am attempting to make this point today because I see so much negativity in our world. I see so many people—good people—who do not accept the fact that they are good. I see so many people who prefer to look down, rather than up; who prefer to frown, rather than smile.

I recall once hearing a young college student refer to himself as "a walking graveyard," and I've often thought that he was speaking for a generation that was succumbing to an epidemic of self-hatred. That is not the way God intended things to be. It may indeed be evidence of progress being made by Satan, the enemy of our human nature, who is surely out to get us, to trap us in a condition of under-confidence and self-loathing. This is surely not the way God intended it to be. What did God intend? Take another look at this morning's Gospel story. Hear once again the words of God breaking out from the heavens and speaking down through the centuries to each one of us: "This is my beloved son, my beloved daughter. My favor surely rests on him, on her."

And have the courage to count yourself in that favored group. God's favor surely rests on you. So wake up to that very positive and encouraging reality; and start living the upbeat Christian life that is—by virtue of your own baptism—God's gift to you.

III
Lent

. . . .

14

First Sunday of Lent

Genesis 2:7–9, 3:1–7; Psalm 51; Romans 5:12–19; Matthew 4:1–11

WE WERE FOOLED BY THE
WISDOM OF THE SERPENT

In the first reading on this the First Sunday of Lent, you are invited back to the Garden of Eden. Adam and Eve are there. You are invited to reflect on the power of God "who formed" Adam (and you) "out of the clay of the ground" and gave Adam (and you) the "breath of life."

Ponder the wonder of creation this morning; ponder the wonder of yourself! And prepare to ponder a bit later on, the story of our original fall from grace.

This opening reading from the Book of Genesis describes the Garden of Eden with its various animals and trees, including the tree of knowledge of good and evil, and it also mentions the serpent, "the most cunning of all the animals that the Lord God has made." You are permitted to overhear a conversation between the woman—Eve—and the serpent who asked her: "Did God really tell you not to eat from any of the trees in the garden?" And you heard Eve's reply: "We may eat of the fruit of the trees in the garden; it is only about the fruit of the tree in the middle of the garden that God said, 'You shall not eat it or even touch it. Lest you die.'"

There you have the famous prohibition that God imposed on Adam and Eve, not to eat the fruit of the tree of knowledge of good and evil. And there you see the appearance of the serpent, and with the serpent, temptation enters the story. The serpent (a consummate liar) says to Eve (you can almost hear a snicker in his voice), "You certainly will not die! No, God knows well that the moment you eat of it you will be like gods who know what is good and what is bad."

Eve was tempted. Scripture says she "saw that the tree was good for food (temptation to evil always comes under the appearance of good), pleasing to the eyes (notice that visual attraction is present), and desirable for gaining wisdom" (here is the temptation to power and pride). And how does Eve respond? Scripture says, "So she took some of its fruit and ate it; and she also gave some to her husband, who was with her, and he ate it." There you have it—the original sin, the first fall, the loss of innocence. Scripture says: "Then the eyes of both of them were opened, and they realized that they were naked; so they sewed fig leaves together and made loincloths for themselves."

This is a world-famous story, a story that has come down to us through the ages, a story that found its way into the inspired writings of God's revelation. And the point of the story is to relate to us that there is evil in the world and as a result of the first encounter of human beings (our first parents) with the forces of evil (embodied here in the serpent, "the most cunning of all the animals" that God created), innocence has been lost and we, the descendants of Adam and Eve, have inherited all the vulnerabilities that are the effects of their original sin.

Theologians have discussed and debated over the centuries the nature of the first sin—a sin of pride, a sin of disobedience, a sin of overreach, uncontrolled desire, breaking out of bounds. Shame accompanied that first sin; hence the fig leaves and loincloths. Regret sets in and, with regret, the painful awareness of having been fooled.

"We were fooled by the wisdom of the serpent," St. Augustine once said, "but we were saved by the foolishness of God."

I invite you today—this First Sunday of the season we call Lent, the time the Church provides for reflection, repentance, and reparation— I invite you today, dear friends, to consider the "wisdom of the serpent" that sets traps that pull us into sin, and also to ponder the reality of "divine foolishness" in the work of salvation that frees us from sin. As you will see, these are countercultural ideas, especially the notion of divine foolishness; so prepare yourselves to see things a bit differently today, to notice evil under the appearance of good (the "wisdom of the serpent') and to recognize that what the world regards as weakness may indeed be God's power (the "divine foolishness") at work in our lives.

In the second reading that you just heard—from Paul's Letter to the Romans—you were reminded that spiritual death came to us all through the sin of one man—Adam—but that through another man's death, the death of Jesus, "acquittal and life" came to all. Elsewhere in Paul's writings (not in the portion included in this Mass), you will find the Apostle saying, "The message of the cross is complete absurdity to those who are headed for ruin, but to us who are experiencing salvation it is the power of God" (1 Cor 1:18). According to Paul, "God turned the wisdom of this world into folly" (v. 20) and "it pleased God to save those who believe through the absurdity of the preaching of the gospel" (v. 22). Folly? Absurdity? What's that all about?

Well, think about your Christian Gospel for a moment. You believe, because Jesus said so, that you can find your life by losing it. You think it is better to give that to receive. You "turn the other cheek" after someone strikes you. You are willing to run after the fellow who steals your cloak just to let him have your shirt. You not only love your neighbor as you love yourself (the Old Law), but you are willing to "lay down your life" for your neighbor (the New Commandment). The Gospel instructs you not to be possessed by your possessions, to love those who hate you, to forgive those who injure you. This is surely not the wisdom of the world; and it can strike you, in reflective moments like these, that what the Good News of Jesus Christ expects you to be and do is more than a bit absurd, and foolish by any worldly measure.

How about the "wisdom of the serpent?" What's that all about? Where do you see that at work in the world? Well, a good place to start looking is in the advertising you see every day—in newspapers, magazines; on billboards, television, the Internet; and in the values highlighted and celebrated in so much of your entertainment. The serpent is really busy there—convincing people that to have is to be, that greed is good, that power beats poverty any day, that the easy life is the good life. Advertising has a quite legitimate role in communicating information about products or services we might want to purchase. But advertising can become an instrument of the serpent when it convinces fat people that they are worthless, old people that they are redundant, and poor people that they have no hope. Eve was the first, but certainly not the last, human to be taken in by visual attraction—that fruit looked really good.

And notice in today's Gospel story how the serpent, Satan—the enemy of our human nature—went after Jesus by hitting direct points of vulnerability: his hunger after forty days of fasting; his potential deficit of self-confidence that could be overcome by legions of angels coming to care for him; and his possible interest in power and possessions—"the kingdoms of the world in their magnificence." But Jesus would have none of that. Keeping his will aligned with the will of his Father was his only concern; it was also his roadmap for the mission he came to fulfill.

And so it can be with you. Think alignment during Lent—alignment of your will with the divine will. Think wisdom during Lent—the wisdom of the serpent and that divine wisdom that may look foolish in the eyes of the world. And think foolishness during Lent, the kind of foolishness represented in the ashes you had placed on your forehead last Wednesday, the kind of foolishness that the Gospel requires of all believers who know, through faith, that if they are sufficiently foolish to separate themselves from the values of this world, they will be secure in achieving, by God's good grace, the rewards of the world to come.

15

Second Sunday of Lent

Genesis 12:1–4a; Psalm 33; 2 Timothy 1:8b–10; Matthew 17:1–9

BEAR YOUR SHARE OF HARDSHIP

On this transfiguration Sunday, I want to take for my text the opening verse in today's second reading, the selection from the Second Letter of Paul to Timothy: "Beloved: Bear your share of hardship for the gospel with the strength that comes from God."

The transfiguration story is there to offer you assurance that there is a strength that can and will come to you from God. That's the point of this striking experience in the life of Jesus, who was transfigured in the presence of his close friends Peter, James, and John, so that they could hear God voice his approval and affirm with blinding light his "beloved Son" in whom God was "so well pleased." By extension, the disciples could apply those affirmative words to themselves. God would be with them. God would be pleased with them in their journey with Jesus. Just as God would be with and affirmative of Jesus in his darkest hour on Calvary, so God would be present to and affirmative of these followers of Christ in their darkest hours.

They failed to hang onto that reassuring message, as you know. When things got really rough, they fled, they deserted their leader.

The dark hours will come to us all. We never want to conclude that God is not there with us in the darkness, in the hardship. That's why it might be helpful on this Second Sunday of Lent to pause on our Lenten journey and reflect on Paul's words to Timothy: "Bear your share of hardship for the gospel with the strength that comes from God."

Let's unpack that sentence and reassemble it in three parts or points: (1) "your share of hardship"; (2) "for the gospel"; and (3) "the strength that comes from God."

1. You have to expect a share of hardship in your life. It is part of the human condition. We want to think that on every go-round we'll grab the brass ring. It just doesn't work out that way. Not that God is there waiting and wanting to punish you. Not at all. Nor is God forgetting you when setbacks come your way (any more than he was forgetful or unmindful of his own Son when hardships, gross injustice, and unimaginable suffering came Christ's way). Jesus suffered. Don't think for a minute that he "suffered with a smile." Look around you at the Stations of the Cross; no smiling Jesus there. He suffered, however, with love, with conviction, with commitment. He suffered for our redemption, for you and me. He died so that we could live. And he lived the pattern that we call the Paschal Mystery, moving through suffering to glory, through death to life, through defeat to victory. And so can you, regardless of whether your sufferings are great or small, regardless of whether your defeats are major or minor. So bear your share of hardship and join your hardships with the hardships of Jesus for the salvation of the world.

2. St. Paul would have you bear your share of hardship "for the gospel." What might this mean in practical terms? Gospel values are not the dominant values that define contemporary culture. If you commit yourself to following Christ in this culture, you will be on a countercultural journey all through life. You will suffer at times because of your commitment to Gospel values. You may be ridiculed. You may be less "successful" in business dealings, not necessarily so, but there will be times when your Christian ethic will not let you cut a corner or take an unfair gain.

   There will certainly be times when your moral convictions will be at variance with the casual or even non-existent sexual standards of the dominant culture. Your faith-based commitment to justice, veracity, integrity, and compassion will have you communicating in a foreign language with many you meet every day.

Hardship will come your way precisely because of your commitment to the Gospel. Paul knew that and said so to Timothy. If your commitment to the Gospel is not noticeable, if it is indiscernible to others, if your spirituality and religious commitment are so plain vanilla that your life is, for all practical purposes, the life of an unbeliever, you will not experience hardship "for the gospel," you'll experience something worse. You will experience meaninglessness and purposelessness. You will drift. If you refuse to lose your life, so to speak, in the spirit of the Gospel, you will never find your life and the full measure of meaning that God intends you to have. You will never experience what I take for my third point this morning, "the strength that comes from God."

3. God knows how weak each one of us is. But only you can know how strong you are when you entrust your life to God. How are you to bear hardship that comes your way because of your commitment to the Gospel? Paul tells you how: "with the strength that comes from God." You know God exists, that's a given; you take it on faith. You know that God is strong, all-powerful. Now Paul wants you to know that the strength of God is there for you, at your side, whenever you need it, especially in hardship and suffering.

Lent is leading toward Easter. Darkness is moving toward light. Defeat is just a delay on the way to victory. You are headed toward victory and you can count on God's strength to bear you up along the way.

And we all know we should be "doing something" for Lent, some small self-sacrifice, some self-denial. It is reparation time—reparation for sin, my own and the sins of others. It is also preparation time, and my voluntary self-restraint, self-denial, and self-control can help me prepare the way for closer union with the risen Lord. But often the most valuable penance, the most effective Lenten observance is simply putting up with the limits in my life, with the hardships that come my way by virtue of my age, health, or circumstances. Putting up with it all, with or without a smile!

You don't have to be a hero to be a true disciple of Christ, a Christian. You just have to be faithful. And your faithfulness may be rewarded from time to time with a transfiguration experience and with a sense of closeness to Jesus. But more often than not you're going to be walking by faith, not light. You're going to be struggling with the hardship of doubt. But remember doubt is not denial, and doubt can never disqualify you from the community of believers. It just makes your journey of faith more difficult.

So hang in there with your Lenten resolutions. And if you have no Lenten resolution, think now about what you might want to do. Don't quit. Don't give up. Die a little to yourself so that an Easter resurrection may be a personal reality for you. "Beloved: Bear your share of hardship for the gospel with the strength that comes from God."

That strength will always be there for you. You can count on it.

16

Third Sunday of Lent

Exodus 17:3–7; Psalm 95; Romans 5:1–2, 5–8; John 4:5–42

WATER AS A METAPHOR FOR GRACE

There's a lot of water in today's readings—water from the rock of Horeb in the reading from Exodus (and that rock is understood to prefigure Jesus, from whose side water and blood flowed when he was hung on the cross); water is there by implication in the reading from Romans where St. Paul speaks of "the love of God [being] poured out into our hearts through the Holy Spirit"; and finally, in the selection from the Gospel of John, you have the water in Jacob's well.

"If you [only] knew the gift of God," says Jesus to the woman at the well, "and who is saying to you, 'Give me a drink,' you would have asked him and he would have given you living water." Living water. What a wonderful metaphor for grace, for the reality of divine life and love within us, within each one of you—living water.

Living water is fresh, flowing, vitalizing, refreshing. Nothing stagnant about living water. Think of what your physical life would be like without water. You will, upon reflection, quickly conclude that there could be no physical life without water; not just stagnation, but death is there in the absence of water. Water is essential for physical life—not just for drinking and bathing, but irrigating, growth-producing water is essential if physical life, yours and that of the croplands, woodlands, and grasslands around you, is to be sustained. You cannot live without water.

Now think about the order of grace, the spiritual order where you live in the love of God. Without grace, without the "living water" Jesus mentioned to the Samaritan woman, your soul would be a parched arid wasteland; your spirit would die. "If you [only] knew the gift of

God," says Jesus to you today as he said to the Samaritan woman centuries ago, "If you [only] knew the gift of God," the gift of grace in your life, how thrilled and grateful you would be.

Think of the qualities of physical water, say, lake water, in your everyday world. Think, for instance, of how lake water seeks its own level. And then consider how living water, the grace poured out be God into your soul, puts you on a certain level with its source, with divine life itself. By God's gift (you are not God, of course, but) you are sanctified, divinized, put on a level of friendship with God, the source of your living water. And at that level you can converse with God just as easily as the Samaritan woman at the well conversed with Jesus.

Think of how fresh water in the brooks, streams, and rivers of your experience follows a pervasive passage through the earth and runs down toward the oceans. Then think of how grace has been following you, living streams of divine love following you, intertwining itself in your daily life, irrigating your spirit, satisfying a deep spiritual thirst within you all your life long. "If you [only] knew the gift of God."

Monsignor Ronald Knox said it well years ago: "Real water is the grace of God from heaven. The clearest, coolest, purest water in the world is just a shadow, a copy of the living stream that flows through the City of God. Grace does not remind Christ of water; water, as we see in the incident at the Well, reminds him of grace" (*Pastoral Sermons*, pp. 335–336).

Think of how ocean water crashes on the shore in waves. That water is salty, sharp to the taste. Those waves are high and often rough. So think of the reality of the challenge, and sometimes the bitterness, associated with grace. Grace rolls and sometimes rushes onto your shore; it challenges you.

Speaking now theologically, not metaphorically, grace is the mystery of God's living presence within you. Take a moment or more today to reflect on the meaning of grace and on the centrality of grace in your spiritual life. Piet Fransen, a Dutch theologian once wrote: "A long list of terms could be prepared to indicate the many ways in which grace, from within, draws and attunes us to God; theology has done so in the past. The reality of grace, however, remains always essentially one and the same thing: an ever purer love for God, offspring of God's own love for us. It is of the utmost importance that we realize this. Only in this light does the technical theology of grace become intelligible and reveal its meaning for our personal life" (*Divine Grace and Man*, p. 80).

Let me conclude on a practical, environmental note, which is also related to the theology of stewardship. We experience frequent droughts in our country now. When and where that happens rainfall is light; snowfall is virtually nonexistent in those areas and thus there is no snow pack to melt and give us water. We know we have to conserve. In our day conservation can be a Lenten sacrifice as well as another form of the practice of stewardship.

And in light of what I've said this morning about water as a metaphor for grace, give some spiritual thought to the possibility of drought in the spiritual life in our world today. Pray for rain in the order of nature and in the order of grace! May God continue to be generous to us as he pours out his love and blessings, like water, upon us all!

17

Fourth Sunday of Lent

1 Samuel 16:1, 6–7, 10–13; Psalm 23; Ephesians 5:8–14; John 9:1–41

DARKNESS AND LIGHT; BLINDNESS AND SIGHT

The Church invites us on this Fourth Sunday of Lent to consider light and darkness, as well as human blindness and the gift of sight. Both practically and metaphorically it is a healthy Lenten exercise to think about light and darkness in our lives, even to imagine for a moment that we are blind, only to be able to rejoice more fully in the gift of sight.

Let me organize this homily around the second reading you heard from the Letter to the Ephesians and then the story of the man born blind who was cured of his blindness by Jesus, as you heard in the Gospel reading from St. John. First we'll consider light and darkness; next the restoration of sight.

In the reading from the Letter to the Ephesians, you were reminded that "you were once darkness, but now you are light in the Lord." The text does not say you are *in the light* of the Lord; no, it says you *are light*" in the Lord. What might that mean? Light in the Lord implies a relationship between you and the Lord.

The Lord is light; indeed the Lord is, as Psalm 27 puts it, "my light and my salvation." And the psalmist draws from that inspired assertion this encouraging conclusion, "whom do I fear?" With the Lord dwelling within you and enlightening you, you have nothing to fear.

There was a time—before your baptism—when you were indeed in darkness, as was the case with the Ephesians before they heard and believed the good news. But with baptism, they and you became illuminated with the life and light of Jesus Christ. There may have been other times between then and now when you chose to turn away from the light, to extinguish the light of Christ within you, and to revert to darkness. But here you are, at this moment, drawn by God's grace into the light. Note again that Paul was telling the Ephesians (and through them, telling you) that you "are light." So again, I have to ask: what might that mean?

It seems to me that Paul is saying that the follower of Christ in an enlightened person, a person who has light within, a person who exudes light, a person who not only reflects the light of Christ but who can illumine his or her part of the world and thus assist others in finding their way out of the darkness into the light. How the world needs that spiritual illumination today!

Darkness suggests discouragement. Darkness implies sin. Darkness offers a refuge for sin and shame. There is a fearsome dimension of darkness—you may have experienced that fear personally. But God wants this world to be free of fear, so God gives to the world the light of Christ and, through you who accept Christ as your savior, God releases spiritual light, encouragement, and hope in your corner of the world. Almost without knowing it, you are providing light that can help overcome darkness. And that is God's work in you. You can think of it as God being "at work" within you.

When lights go on in your home or here in church, for example, you ordinarily do not think of where that light originates, where it is generated. There is, of course, a power company that provides it; the artificial light around you has a source. And so it is in the spiritual life. Simply by living a good life, you can generate light for others. You can be a source of spiritual illumination for others, by willing to be so, by uniting your prayer, your good works, your will with the will of God, you can work along with God for the salvation of the world. That happens not just through your Lenten sacrifice; it happens all year round.

Now let's consider the Gospel story, the cure of the man born blind. Blindness is, by definition, darkness. You can imagine what it is like. You can simply close your eyes and imagine that you are blind. But you are also free to open your eyes and see again.

The man born blind was not free simply to open his eyes. He had to await the working of divine power on his behalf. Jesus came across him, the Gospel says, "as Jesus passes by." The disciples who were walking along with Jesus were intrigued by this man and asked their Lord whether the sins of his parents had caused the unfortunate man's blindness. That was a common misperception then and remains so in our own day. No, Jesus assured his disciples, the sins of this man's father were not the cause of his blindness. "Neither he nor his parents sinned," said Jesus; "it is so that the works of God might be made visible through him."

In other words, the permissive will of God allowed a natural phenomenon, blindness, in order to set the stage for a supernatural act—a cure that would witness to the presence and power of God in this world. But how was this power to become engaged? How was the cure brought about? Jesus was moved by pity for the man; he was also moved by a desire to show forth God's power and presence in the world. So he engaged in ritual activity much like the sacramental rituals that are familiar to you. In this case, Jesus made mud with his own saliva and smeared the mud on the man's eyes. Then he told him to wash, which the man did, and he came back able to see. His obedience to instruction proved to be part of the ritual. His cure, however, caused quite a stir in the community. First, people doubted that the cured man was in fact the same man who had been born blind. Next, the Pharisees—ever so righteous and scrupulous observers of the law—complained that this miracle was performed on the Sabbath and thus violated the prohibition of work on the Sabbath.

The man, now a focus of ridicule and controversy, was thrown out bodily from the community. But Jesus sought him out and engaged him in a dialogue of faith. "Do you believe in the Son of Man?" "Who is he, sir, that I may believe in him?" "You have seen him," Jesus replied, "and the one speaking with you is he."

And the man professed his faith in Jesus. The cure drew the desired response—an act of faith.

So, here we are on the Fourth Sunday of Lent. We can pretend to be blind simply by closing our eyes. We can pretend to be cured, simply by opening them again. Or, with eyes wide open, we can look with the eye of faith at Jesus—present, but not seeable in our midst, in one another; present and audible, but not touchable in the readings just proclaimed from Scripture; present, but not visible or audible under the appearance of bread and wine on our altar—we can see him with the eye of faith and we can say today, *Credo*, "I believe."

That act of faith brings us out of the darkness and into the light. That act of faith represents a cure for our blindness and brings us into the light. By that act of faith, we become light, and because of our presence in the world, the world is a brighter place, that much closer to finding its way home to its creator. So, believe, and give thanks to God for the faith that is yours.

18

Fifth Sunday of Lent

Ezekiel 37:12–14; Psalm 130; Romans 8:8–11; John 11:1–45

LAZARUS

"'Lazarus, come out!' The dead man came out, tied hand and foot with burial bands, and his face was wrapped in a cloth." Notice, dear friends, the difference between this account of the dead Lazarus coming back to life, and the account you will find of the Easter event, the resurrection of Jesus, in the Gospel of John. There you will read in chapter 20 a description of what Peter and John found when they ran out to the tomb early on Easter morning: "When Simon Peter arrived…he went into the tomb and saw the burial cloths there, and the cloth that had covered his head, not with the burial cloths but rolled up in a separate place."

Lazarus was out of the tomb but bound hand and foot with burial wrappings and his face was still covered with the burial cloth. Jesus, by contrast, was free of the burial cloths; they were left behind. Why? Because never again would death touch him; he would never return to the grave. But Lazarus, raised miraculously from the grave, would still be in need of burial cloths; he would have to die again before entering eternal life. "So Jesus said to them, 'Untie him and let him go.'" He was untied; he was let go. He walked again on this earth but only for a while; eventually he died. We walk on this earth only for a while; eventually we shall die.

There is something in this Lazarus event that holds a mirror up before you. You were raised from the dead, first in baptism, when you were sacramentally and symbolically plunged into the death of Jesus so that, with Jesus, you could rise to walk in newness of life—the life of grace. You've been raised again, many times perhaps, from the death of serious sin, to walk renewed—unbound and free. You know the feeling, I suspect. You've been untied and released from sin, but possessed as you are of a mortal human nature, you remain in need of burial cloths. You, like Lazarus, will surely die, and you, like Lazarus, should be wildly grateful for your return now to life—to the grace, friendship, and love of God that you may well have lost, by your own foolish choice, sometime in the past.

There is so much more in this story to ponder, to savor really. Let me highlight just two of the many phrases that you could dwell on prayerfully, meditatively today. The first is a puzzler, something of a riddle: "Now Jesus loved...Lazarus, [s]o when he heard that he was ill, he remained for two days in the place where he was." Loved him? Why didn't Jesus rush out to comfort Mary and Martha, the sisters of Lazarus; why didn't he run out to raise Lazarus back to life? He loved him, so he remained and did nothing for two days!

Think about that in anticipation of your next illness. Indeed, have the courage to think about that now in anticipation of your final illness. "Master, the one you love is ill." That fact will come to his attention someday in your regard. And just as when he heard that Lazarus was ill, so too in your case the story may be one of no immediate response, no discernible move in your direction. "So when he heard that [you were ill], he remained for two days [a figurative period of time] where he was."

When he is silent, you must never conclude that he is absent. When healing and full recovery elude you, as they most certainly one day will, you must never conclude that he is not with you. Yours is a relationship of faith and friendship; he can never be anything to you but faithful. He will never, ever, disappoint you. When your fears deepen and your hopes dim, you are simply getting closer to his eternal embrace.

The second point I'd like you to ponder is wrapped up in the simple sentence, "And Jesus wept." Yes, he wept. He was soft; he was human; he had tear ducts that worked. Scholars speculate whether the weeping reflected a bit of anger over the obtuseness of some of his followers, over their inability to see things through the eye of faith, but I don't think so. I think the tears were tears of friendship.

A friend was gone. There hadn't been a chance to say good-bye. It happens often between friends. One is gone; the other is left behind to weep. "And Jesus wept." That's your friend weeping. He's your savior. He would have wept for you had you been around when he walked the earth. He can't weep for you now (nor, by the way, can anything you do or fail to do make him weep now) now that he lives in glory. But with all the warmth and sensitivity that any human could possibly have, he loves you now and he will love you always, no matter what!

It is quietly amusing to me when I see someone who has just recovered from a serious illness or who had a close call with a life-threatening accident and I ask, "How're you doing?" And the reply comes: "Not bad, considering the alternative!" That's amusing, I say, because it raises the obvious question: "Yes, but have you ever really considered the alternative, have you considered how unimaginably great that alternative will be?"

Lazarus was given more time. What do you suppose he did with it? Each one of us, in one way or another, has been given more time. What are we doing with it? If you were seriously ill, this prayer from the Mass for the Sick may well have been said for you. The wording dates back before the 2011 reform of the Roman Missal. Notice how it is a plea for your return to health: "God our Father, our help in human weakness, show our sick brothers and sisters the power of your loving care. In your kindness make them well and restore them to your Church." That's the prayer after Communion in the old Mass for the Sick. If you have been restored to health, returned to the Church, you have to ask yourself: for what purpose? What should I now be doing with my time and health to show my gratitude for both?

So here you are back in good health. In some cases, you may have been returned from a near death experience. Like Lazarus, you have the burial cloths as souvenirs. You're going to need them again someday. You can count on eventually wearing them with peace and pride for your journey home to heaven *if* (and it is an important *if*)—if you use your time well in giving praise and thanks to God (as you're doing today in this Eucharist), and if you show your love of God by showing love and generous service to your brothers and sisters in the human community.

I don't have to remind you that it is Lent—a time to exercise self-restraint, self-control, a time for a bit of penance. Many centuries ago, the Lenten observance may well have introduced you to sackcloth and ashes. We don't see any of that around us today. But we do receive our ashes on the opening day of Lent—Ash Wednesday. Now, with the eye of faith, we might see to it that there is a place in our wardrobes for those burial cloths. Lazarus happily hung his up when he came back to life and we might presume that he spent his days giving thanks to God and reaching out to those in need. We too should be grateful and helpful, as best we can, and thus make the most of the precious time that is ours.

19

Passion Sunday (Palm Sunday)

Isaiah 50:4–7; Psalm 22; Philippians 2:6–11;
Matthew 26:14—27:66

"MY GOD, MY GOD, WHY HAVE YOU ABANDONED ME?"

All of us, from time to time, have a tendency to think that God may have abandoned us—we think we are left us to our own resources, unable to cope, alone and vulnerable. Apparently, Jesus knew that feeling.

Matthew's passion narrative, which was just proclaimed in your hearing in this Palm Sunday liturgy, repeats the poignant expression, "My God, my God, why have you abandoned me?" And we are left with the puzzle of trying to figure out how the Son of God, our Lord Jesus Christ—true God and true Man—could possibly have experienced the psychological abandonment that produced that outcry. We can only ponder the mystery, but the very pondering of those words can give us strength.

Today's first reading, taken from the prophet Isaiah, puts the following words on the lips of the Suffering Servant of Yahweh: "The Lord God is my help, therefore I am not disgraced; I have set my face like flint, knowing that I shall not be put to shame" (Isa 50:7). Deep down in his heart of hearts, Jesus knew this; he knew that he would not be abandoned, but in some mysterious way an awareness of that fact escaped his consciousness at that dreadful moment on the cross. His face was set like flint, suggesting the presence of unshakable faith, but the consciousness of God's presence was mysteriously absent.

Elsewhere in the Old Testament, in the Book of Genesis, the story is related of how Abraham was instructed to sacrifice his son Isaac and, although deeply troubled and confused, remained obedient to the Lord's command. He proved himself to be up to the test. As you will recall from the Genesis account, "Abraham took the wood for the holocaust and laid it on his son Isaac's shoulders, while he himself carried the fire and the knife. As the two walked on together, Isaac spoke to his father Abraham, 'Father!' he said. 'Yes, son,' he replied. Isaac continued, 'Here are the fire and the wood, but where is the sheep for the holocaust? 'Son,' Abraham answered, 'God himself will provide the sheep for the holocaust.' Then the two continued going forward" (22:6–8).

They continued going forward.

God hovered over them every step of the way unseen by them; they were unaware. They "continued going forward" and not only the eye of God but the love of God hovered over them every step of the way. Eventually, the voice of the Lord's messenger broke through: "Abraham, Abraham…do not lay your hand on the boy….Do not the least thing to him." "Again the Lord's messenger called to Abraham from heaven and said: 'I swear by myself, says the Lord, that because you acted as you did in not withholding from me your beloved son, I will bless you abundantly'" (Gen 22:12).

And something similar happened with Jesus on his way of the cross, which was retraced for you in the reading of the passion narrative in this Palm Sunday liturgy. The love of God hovered over him every step of the way. Momentary expressions of that love broke through, for example, in the intervention of Simon of Cyrene whose shoulder eased for a few moments the burden of the cross weighing heavily on the shoulders of Jesus. But once nailed to the cross, he was alone, left to die. Abandoned. Or so he seemed to think when he cried out "My God, my God, why have you abandoned me?"

Perhaps you know the feeling. Perhaps those words have been, at one time or another, your own. Well, as you walk the way of the cross in companionship and loving memory with Jesus today, be grateful to the courageous Christ who set his face like flint and walked on in a faith that did not fail him, toward a fate that can make sense only when viewed in the framework of the divine foolishness. Ask for the grace to see that any segment of the way of the cross that you are asked to walk during your sojourn here on earth is the sure and certain way to eternal glory.

You are called to live and die under the banner of the cross. The full liturgical observance of this Holy Week that begins today will help you see the wisdom in the divine foolishness outlined for you today in the reading of the passion narrative according to St. Matthew.

IV
Triduum

. . . .

20

Holy Thursday, Mass of the Lord's Supper

Exodus 12:1–8, 11–14; Psalm 116;
1 Corinthians 11:23–26; John 13:1–15

"DO YOU UNDERSTAND WHAT I JUST DID FOR YOU?"

Jesus asked a question of his disciples in the reading you just heard from the Gospel of John. Hear him ask each of you that same question this evening at this Mass of the Lord's Supper. He had just finished washing the feet of his disciples and he rejoined them at the supper table and asked: "Do you understand what I just did for you?"

Let those words come through directly to you this evening. Recall the setting. Put yourself in place right there with the disciples and hear Jesus say to you: "Do you understand what I just did for you?"

Well, do you? Do you understand? Do you have any idea of the symbolism of what he just did, of the implications for you in the action you just witnessed?

"You address me as 'Teacher' and 'Lord,'" said Jesus, "and fittingly enough, for that is what I am. But if I washed your feet—I who am Teacher and Lord—then you must wash each other's feet. What I just did was to give you an example: as I have done so you must do" (John 13:15).

In effect, Jesus is saying, "I want to make foot-washers of you all." That sounds strange to us living, as we do, so far removed from the foot-washing culture that was a familiar part of life when Jesus walked our earth. All the more reason that we should pay special attention now. We are called to be foot-washing companions of the Lord. We are called ultimately to lay down our lives for one another (as Jesus says later in John's Gospel), but we are called immediately and daily to be caring companions, facing off with one another in self-denying service, putting the other fellow first, being attentive to the other's needs, loving one another as Jesus loved us.

There you have the implications for us tonight of the action Jesus took on the night before he died. That was also the night on which he instituted the Eucharist, the sacrament and sacrifice of his Body and Blood. We are remembering all of that in this Holy Thursday liturgy. We do it in modern times in an era that is witnessing a decline in Catholic participation in the celebration of the Holy Eucharist. Perhaps tonight we can pray for deeper faith in the mystery of the Eucharist, a deeper awareness that it is indeed the Body and Blood of Christ that we consume at the Table of the Lord, at every Mass. It is nourishment for our souls. It sustains us, the Eucharist, on our journey of faith—week by week, year by year—until we are with the Lord and our other companions in faith forever in eternal life.

We have so much to be grateful for. Getting back to the implications for us of the foot-washing action we have just witnessed, we can show our gratitude to God by caring for the needs of those who, by God's providence, live within reach of our helping—foot-washing—hands.

There is no need for a long homily in this symbolism-rich Holy Thursday liturgy. Let's leave it here along with a resolution to ponder, as the rest of Holy Week unfolds, the action-oriented implications of the signs we see and the words we hear in this special season of the year.

21

Good Friday, the Passion of the Lord

Isaiah 52:13—53:12; Psalm 31; Hebrews 4:14–16; 5:7–9;
John 18:1—19:42

WOMAN, BEHOLD YOUR SON

When Jesus saw his mother and the disciple there whom he loved, he said to his mother, "Woman, behold your son." Then he said to the disciple, "Behold your mother." And from that hour the disciple took her into his home. (John 19:26–27)

Standing, as we are this afternoon, at the foot of the cross—a station, had we been alive on that fateful Friday afternoon, we probably would not have had the courage to take—standing there now in faith, we hear Jesus speak (through John) to us: "Behold, your mother." And we hear him directing her attention to us, saying to her in effect, "Behold your sons and daughters; be mother to them, care for them."

Here, at the foot of the cross on the hill of Calvary, another scene will develop shortly. Another image will emerge. I invite you to take that image to yourself now with your mind's eye, welcome it into memory and imagination. It is the image of the famous Michelangelo masterpiece, the *Pietá*. In that exquisite sculpture you find, carved in marble, a moving representation of pity and sorrow. You see Mary burdened with the weight of her dead Son stretched across her lap. She is burdened with the weight of sorrow and yet at peace as she gazes at the lifeless body of him whose promise extended to her, as well as to you and me, that we were all to learn of him, of his gentleness, of his humility, and with those lessons learned, she (Mary), you and I, all of us, would not find life burdensome. Remember the promise? "Take my yoke upon you and learn from me, for I am meek [gentle] and humble of heart; and you will find rest for yourselves. For my yoke is easy and my burden light" (Matt 11:29).

That was and is a promise of Christ to Mary, his first follower, and to all of us who would follow later, that we would—by knowing and learning from Christ—that we would achieve an abiding sense of peace despite the weight of life's burdens.

In the Christmas season, you saw the image of the Madonna and Child, the young mother and the baby at the beginning of that baby's life on earth. In the *Pietá*, you see the end, the end of an earthly journey of thirty-three years. In this artistic presentation, Mary's son, the Son of God, is once again on her lap.

All who look on Michelangelo's *Pietá* can see how insupportably heavy the body of her dead Son is on Mary's lap. Looking at her sculpted features we can also see how much heavier was the burden in her heart. The genius of Michelangelo combined two life-size figures in one sculpture, carved from one block of marble. Both figures are bathed in tranquility. The mother can see and weep; the Son's eyes are closed in death. The mother can also hope, and the Son, as we now know, did indeed rise again.

Today, dear friends, we gather as a remembering people. We gather also as a people of hope. In the silent sadness of the *Pietá*, we see both hope and the promise of resurrection.

We now find ourselves perhaps yoked and burdened with the cares of life, but we know that by the power of Christ's resurrection, the yoke will become easy, the burden will be lightened through our faith-based participation in the victory of the risen Jesus.

We believe the eternal truth communicated by Paul to the Romans, "If God is for us, who can be against us? ...It is Christ [Jesus] who died, rather, was raised, who also is at the right hand of God, who indeed intercedes for us. What will separate us from the love of Christ?" (Rom 8:31, 34) We answer that question from the depths of our sad but faith-filled hearts with one word: Nothing. Let nothing, we pray, ever separate us from the love of Christ.

It was the love of Christ on the cross that entrusted us to his mother. The love of Christ commended her to us. Her love for us is at work in us today.

"When Jesus saw his mother and the disciple there whom he loved, he said to his mother, 'Woman, behold your son.' Then he said to the disciple, 'Behold, your mother.' And from that hour the disciple took her into his home." Take her to your home. Let her take you to her Son.

An ancient hymn of the Church connects these stations and links them antiphonally with the words, "Have mercy, O lord, have mercy on us."

We give thanks and praise to God on this Good Friday afternoon, that on the first Good Friday afternoon, the woman who was the first disciple of Jesus was there by the cross with him when most of his other disciples had fled; there to comfort him and to receive us; there to hold his body when it was taken down from the cross.

And here now with us, here now to present us to him when we find life burdensome and in need of the rest that only he can give.

22

Easter Vigil

Seven Old Testament Readings; Romans 6:3–11;
then for Year A, Matthew 28:1–10

Contextual Note: This homily was delivered at the first Easter
Vigil following the public disclosure in 2002 of sexual abuse of
children by Catholic clergy in the Archdiocese of Boston.

"DO NOT BE AFRAID"

Confidence is the word for us at this hour: confident reassurance; confidence in ourselves based on an unshakable confidence in our risen
Christ who conquered death and lives in glory; confidence in the
Father who raised his Son Christ from the dead and, who, through his
gift to us in baptism, raises us up as well.

Be confident then. Your baptism releases you, rescues you, raises
you to walk in newness of life. Be confident. And also be profoundly
grateful.

The Church reminds you repeatedly in the Easter liturgy that you
"were buried with Christ in baptism." The word *baptism* means
"plunge." The water of baptism symbolizes not only a cleansing but a
drowning. You drown, you die with Christ in baptism, so that you can
rise with Christ to walk in newness of life—the graced life, God's gift
of grace to you.

The practical conclusion to be drawn from our collective reflection
on the paschal mystery—the mystery of Christ's death and resurrection, the mystery of the Christian passage to life through death—is
this: "Death's not what we're moving toward; it is what we're coming
from!" So be confident at this hour; know that death, the death of sin,
is behind you, and life, eternal life, awaits you.

"Are you unaware," Paul asks you, as his Letter to the Romans asked two thousand years ago, "Are you unaware that we who were baptized into Christ Jesus were baptized into his death? We were indeed buried with him through baptism into death, so that, just as Christ was raised from the dead by the glory of the Father, we too might live in newness of life."

Be confident, then, and listen once again to the angel, the messenger, who as you heard in the Gospel story, approached "Mary Magdalene and the other Mary" and who "rolled back the stone, and sat upon it. His appearance was like lightning and his clothing was white as snow…and he said to the women: 'Do not be afraid! I know that you are seeking Jesus the crucified. He is not here, for he has been raised just as he said. Come and see the place where he lay. Then go quickly and tell his disciples, He has been raised from the dead, and he is going before you to Galilee.'"

Heed those words, dear friends. Let them help to build up your confidence. Believe that Jesus goes before you, indeed has been going before you every moment of your earthly existence, every inch of the way on your pilgrimage of faith. He is with you right now. Be confident. Be not afraid. Be grateful and praise the Lord!

These, as all of us know so painfully and so well, are difficult days in the life of the Catholic Church in America. I have found myself these days often turning over in my heart and prayer words that I recommend now to you to reinforce your Easter confidence. In the fifth chapter of his Letter to the Romans, St. Paul makes this astonishing assertion: "Where sin increased, grace overflowed all the more" (Rom 5:20). Believe that to be true. It is one more way of proclaiming your Easter faith, the faith that bonds us all together now in life and love as a grateful Easter people.

V
Easter

. . . .

23

Easter Sunday

Acts 10:34a, 37–43; Psalm 118; Colossians 3:14; John 20:1–9

"YOU HAVE BEEN RAISED UP IN COMPANY WITH CHRIST"

A lot of Easter wisdom is packed into that short second reading you just heard from the Letter to the Colossians. Read it again when you get home today and notice how it puts you in the resurrection spotlight. "You have been raised up in company with Christ." That's right—you, together with Christ, have been raised up.

What might that possibly mean? It means exactly what it says. You've been raised from the dead.

In the letters written by Paul or the followers of Paul, there are frequent references made to our "death" in the waters of baptism. We symbolically drown in the baptismal waters only to rise again to walk in newness of life—the grace life. That's what the sacrament of baptism did for you. It enabled you to be "raised up in company with Christ." You received what your catechism called the gift of "sanctifying grace." You were transformed from the death of sin to the life of grace and, through baptism, grace is yours in the presence of the indwelling Spirit. Now grace, of course, means gift; and all you can be in your personal resurrection joy is grateful!

As I said, there is a lot of Easter wisdom packed into that short selection you have today from the Letter to the Colossians. Think of yourself in Easter terms. Think of yourself as walking in new life!

Here is how the Letter to the Colossians (3:1–4) sets it up for you: "Since you have been raised up in company with Christ, set your heart on what pertains to higher realms where Christ is seated at God's right hand. Be intent on things above rather than on things of earth. After all, you have died [in baptism]! Your life is hidden now with Christ in God."

Notice those phrases "set your heart" and "be intent." Scripture is holding up a mirror for you on this Easter Sunday and asking you to see where your heart is really set, where your interests really are. And this reading from Colossians invites you to check on the intensity of your commitment to things of the spirit as compared with your attachment to material things.

Another way of looking at all this on Easter Sunday is to ask whether or not you are possessed by your possessions. Are you really free? Have you really risen above earthly attachments or does the weight of worldly concerns hold you down from the full experience of the resurrection joy God intends you to have on this Easter Sunday?

To say that "your life is hidden now with Christ in God" is not to deny that there is a material side to your existence; it is not to deny that you have material needs, and that worldly concerns require your attention. But if "your life is hidden now with Christ in God," you, in companionship with Christ, will keep matter and spirit in balance as you make your way through life and await his coming in glory. "When Christ our life appears," says the Letter to the Colossians, "then you shall appear with him in glory." That's you, the resurrected you, on your way to your full share in Easter glory—the resurrection glory that awaits you is very real and on its way.

That's why I'm suggesting that you personalize this Easter celebration. Recalling the Easter reality in the life of Christ, you can acknowledge that, by the gift of faith, you've been able to pick a winner. But the deeper reality and a source of indescribable Easter joy is the fact that a winner has picked you! This is victory day, this Easter Sunday. The victory is Christ's, of course, but he has chosen to share that victory with us and make winners of us all.

How can you not be glad today? How can you not be grateful?

24

Second Sunday of Easter

Acts 2:42–47; Psalm 118; 1 Peter 1:3–9; John 20:19–31

"THE BRETHREN DEVOTED THEMSELVES TO THE...BREAKING OF BREAD"

The reading from the Acts of the Apostles that the Church proposes today for your post-Easter reflection takes you back to the very beginnings of the life of the early Christian community. As you look left and right and around you in this Eucharistic assembly, you see some evidence, but not very much, of what the writer of Acts saw in the earliest days of our church. As the selection you had from Acts in your first reading today puts it, "The brethren devoted themselves to the apostles' instruction (as you do every Sunday when Scripture is read and homilies are given) and the communal life (you won't find much evidence of that now), to the breaking of bread and the prayers (happily we have that in the Eucharistic elements and the Eucharistic Prayer)."

Here we are, more than two thousand years later, doing essentially the same thing that the earliest disciples of Christ did in remembrance of him. They shared reflections on the Scriptures. They broke the Eucharistic bread together. And they tried to support one another in all their needs.

The earliest description that we have outside the New Testament of what the early believers did when they met on Sundays is preserved for us in a reflection written by St. Justin Martyr in the year 150. He apparently kept something of a diary and recorded one Sunday what had happened earlier that day. It is called his *Apology*. Let me recall portions from memory and paraphrase them for you here: "On the day that is named after the sun," wrote Justin, "we come together from the outlying districts to one of our homes where the "memoirs of the apostles" are read. "And the president of the assembly (the presider) urges all to follow the lessons and good example contained therein. Then the bread and wine are offered and the president of the assembly recites a prayer of thanksgiving to the best of his ability, and those present express their approval by saying Amen." (That, of course, was long before the age of print and the presider had to make it up as he went along!) Justin continues: "Then the gifts over which the prayer has been said are distributed and a portion is set aside to be taken afterwards by the women to those who are sick." (Even back then there were extraordinary ministers of Communion!) "The wealthy, if they wish," wrote Justin, "contribute what they wish and the collection is kept in the custody of the president for later distribution to widows and orphans."

Notice how all the elements of the Sunday Mass, so familiar to all of you today, were present then: the readings from Scripture; the homily; the Eucharistic Prayer of thanksgiving; the same "Amen" that you will recite today at the end of what we call the Canon of the Mass; the distribution of communion; and the never to be omitted collection that is kept in the custody of the president! The application of contributions "for the care of widows and orphans" has been the Church's way since the beginning of describing its commitment to and care for the poor. All of that is still with us.

Let me encourage you to speculate for a moment on where those people are now—those who gathered in the year 150 in the worshipping community that Justin described. It is obvious that they are no longer with us here on earth. But where are they? We can assume that they are "with the Lord" because there they were, Sunday after Sunday, in the channel to salvation that is the community of faith.

If I were to write a description of what we are doing here today and someone came along a few hundred years from now and read it, and asked the same question as to our whereabouts, we know, with the certainty of faith, that we, a couple of hundred years from now, will also be "with the Lord" and remain with him forever!

Take great comfort in that realization, my friends, not presumptuous pride, but quiet comfort in the assurance that only faith can provide. You are right now where you belong, in the channel of salvation that is this Eucharistic assembly. You are on your way home to heaven. You have lots to do before you reach that final destination and you need the nourishment that the Eucharistic meal provides to sustain you in your continuing commitment to faith and good works along the way. But my point at the moment is that you should move along confidently (*con-fide*—"with faith"—is the meaning of that word *confidently*). Yours is not a religion of doom and gloom. Your Sunday worship is (at least it should be!) a celebration of your redemption through the death and resurrection of Jesus.

I wish we had never fallen into what I consider the unfortunate vocabulary of referring to the "Sunday obligation." It should be, in my view, be called the "Sunday celebration," just as those so-called "holy days of obligation" should, I would argue, be called "special days of celebration."

So listen again with grateful hearts to the absolutely thrilling words that you heard just moments ago in today's second reading, taken from the First Letter of Peter (1 Pet 3:1ff):

> Praised be the God and Father of our Lord, Jesus Christ, he who in his great mercy gave us new birth; a birth unto hope which draws its life from the resurrection of Jesus Christ from the dead; a birth to an imperishable inheritance incapable of fading or defilement, which is kept in heaven for you who are guarded with God's power through faith; a birth to a salvation which stands ready to be revealed in the last days.

Just pray, dear friends, for the Easter gift of being able to really hear those words and hold them in your hearts.

25

Third Sunday of Easter

Acts 2:14, 22–33; Psalm 16; 1 Peter 1:17–21; Luke 24:13–35

ON THE ROAD

It was back in 1957 that a novel called *On the Road* by Jack Kerouac first appeared. He was the voice of the so-called Beat Generation. And he made the "road" something of a metaphor for drifting and purposelessness. When you had nowhere to go, you went "on the road."

We have an "on the road" story in today's Gospel. It is a New Testament favorite of many people—a warm and wonderful story of Easter faith. It is important for us this morning to notice that Jerusalem is mentioned at the beginning of this story, the same Jerusalem that is the dateline for news stories coming to us on occasion with reports of terrorism, suicide bombings, and war between Israelis and Palestinians. What is happening in the troubled Middle East these days is happening in the region where this Gospel story is set. Think about that. Jesus walked the same roads that the terrorists and combatants have walked and are walking today in what we know as the Holy Land.

This is an Easter story. The point of the story is to show you that your Easter faith must be understood as faith in the resurrected Jesus. It is a story, by the way, of special significance to catechists because that is exactly what Jesus does as he walks along the way with these two disciples who were not members of his original band of twelve apostles. They need to be catechized. So he catechizes them about himself, his teachings, his death, and his resurrection. And he sets their hearts afire with his interpretation of the Hebrew Scriptures. A great catechist!

Luke's on-the-road story has four parts.

First, there is a meeting of these two discouraged, dejected disciples with Jesus as they walk between Jerusalem and Emmaus. They meet

Jesus but do not recognize him. He just falls in step with them. He has risen now, and he just shows up from time to time.

Second, there is a conversation as they walk along. The disciples were talking between themselves, and Christ enters into that conversation: "What are you discussing as you walk along?" he asks them. One of them, named Cleopas (we do not have the name of the other; it might have been the wife of Cleopas, we just don't know) says: "Are you the only visitor to Jerusalem who is unaware of what happened there these past few days?" And Cleopas goes on to relate the whole story only to be met at the end with these words of Jesus: "Oh, how foolish you are! How slow of heart to believe all that the prophets spoke! Was it not necessary that the Christ should suffer these things and enter into his glory?" Then, Luke tells us, Jesus began with Moses and all the prophets and interpreted for these two disciples whatever referred to him in all the Scriptures. What a lesson that must have been!

The third part of the story is the meal. Jesus acted as if he was going to continue on the way, but they persuaded him to come in with them to the house where they were planning to stay in Emmaus. "Stay with us, for it is nearly evening and the day is almost over." So he stayed with them. Here's the best part of the story. "And it happened that, while he was with them at table, he took bread, said the blessing, broke it, and gave it to them. With that their eyes were opened and they recognized him, but he vanished from their sight." They had not been at the Last Supper, these two disciples, but what he did here at the table was like what he did then. "He took bread, said the blessing, broke it, and gave it to them." In the midst of all this, their eyes were opened. They recognized him in the breaking of the bread.

Now ask yourself. Did the bread that was broken and passed around symbolize for them the Jesus they knew who permitted himself to be beaten and broken bodily on the cross for the salvation of others? Did the table ritual remind them of other meals they had enjoyed with him so they saw him in this one? Or did he simply break through into their consciousness at this special and sacred moment? We don't know. We can only speculate. But we can hope that as we remember him in the breaking of our Eucharistic bread every Sunday, we too may recognize him and experience a closeness to him similar to that experienced by these disciples in this beautiful story.

Jesus vanished from their sight, but they had seen him and recognized him, and Luke's account has them saying to each other, "Were not our hearts burning within us while he spoke to us on the way and opened the Scriptures to us?"

The fourth part of the story is the joyous return to Jerusalem by these two energized disciples. They caught up with the eleven apostles and, as Luke tells us, they "recounted what had taken place on the way and how he was made known to them in the breaking of the bread." There is happiness and hope here. There is Easter faith here. They believe, as you and I are called to believe, that Jesus is indeed Lord and the Father truly raised him from the dead.

You hear the word *discernment* mentioned from time to time in homilies and in retreats and spiritual direction. Discernment begins with feelings. God communicates with you through your feelings, and your job is to discern, to sort out your feelings to see what is of God there, and where perhaps God is drawing you; in what direction does God want you to move and to decide? In this Gospel story, the disciples say, "Were not our hearts burning within us while he spoke to us on the way…?" Hearts burning within us—feelings; a sense experience of being drawn toward God, of being in God's presence.

Pray today that you might experience that from time to time. Ask yourself what your gut, your heart, your feelings might be telling you in a given situation, and consider that those feelings may indeed be God's will working its way into your consciousness.

So get in touch with your feelings—with that heart burning within you—as one way of getting in touch with God. If, as may well be the case, you feel flat, maybe even numb—no feeling at all—ask God to communicate himself to you through your feelings. It may not last for long. Their hearts burned within them for a little while, a special privileged moment or two. May that same gift be yours, and may you learn from him as you meet him on the road, along the way of your own faith journey, for he does indeed walk with you in your journey of faith.

26

Fourth Sunday of Easter

Acts 2:14a, 36–41; Psalm 23; 1 Peter 2:20b–25; John 10:1–10

Contextual note: This homily was first delivered when both the Enron crisis in business and the clergy sex abuse crisis in Boston were in the headlines.

THE SHEPHERD LEADER

This is Good Shepherd Sunday and I'd like to suggest that we think and pray today about shepherd leadership.

You've heard, I suspect, the expression, *Servant Leadership*. It is the title of a fine book by Robert Greenleaf, who challenged leaders in all walks of life to regard themselves as servants. You can appreciate how "servant leadership" is a congenial term for leadership in our Church, an appropriate ideal for all who minister in the Church, especially for pastors, bishops, cardinals, and the Holy Father.

The first decade of the twenty-first century has brought difficult days for both leaders and followers in the Catholic Church. They've also been difficult days for leaders in the business community, in education, in government, and in international affairs. Leaders, if they want to be servant leaders, and especially if they want to be authentic shepherd leaders, must be available, accountable, and vulnerable.

The Good Shepherd, as you know from Scripture, is prepared to give his life for his sheep. That's shepherd leadership.

The shepherd leader is there for and with the followership: "the sheep hear his voice." The shepherd leader knows his own: "The shepherd calls his own sheep by name." "[H]e walks ahead of them, and the sheep follow him, because they recognize his voice."

You get a fuller picture of the Good Shepherd if you read the verses before and after today's selection from the Gospel of John. Perhaps when you go home today you could take a few minutes to read the entire tenth chapter of John's Gospel, and you'll see what I mean. In any case, in this segment, Jesus compares himself to the gate of the sheepfold. "I am the gate. Whoever enters through me will be saved, and will come in and go out and find pasture....I came that they might have life and have it more abundantly." That is what shepherd leaders are called to do—to enable their followers to live fuller lives, to have life and have it more abundantly.

In the present crisis of leadership confronting the Catholic Church in the United States, a helpful lesson might be learned from two contemporary business writers. Note that they are writing about business leaders. One way to stop a business leader in his or her tracks, write consultants Robert Goffee and Gareth Jones, is to ask: "Why Should Anyone Be Led by You?" That question is the title of an article these observers wrote for the *Harvard Business Review* (September–October 2000). "Without fail," say the authors, "the response is a sudden, stunned hush. All you can hear are knees knocking."

The question is a good one to put to anyone in a leadership position anywhere. How would a cardinal, bishop, or pastor respond today? The reply has to be something more substantial than, "I've been assigned." Leadership implies voluntary followership. If you're the leader, why should anybody follow?

Goffee and Jones give a backward glance through history and acknowledge that there have been widely accepted leadership traits and styles. But they change over time. Today, these authors argue, the times require that "Leaders should let their weaknesses be known. By exposing a measure of vulnerability, they make themselves approachable and show themselves to be human." Today's leaders, say these authors, have to adapt to "endless contingencies" while making decisions suited to a particular situation. They have to be "good situation sensors [able to] collect and interpret soft data."

Why should knees knock when a leader is asked, "Why should anyone be led by you?" If the so-called leader has specialized in unavailability, unaccountability, and presumed invulnerability, the question could be quite discomfiting. Those in leadership positions in our

Church today should be wise enough to ask themselves why they are there. And those who constitute the followership can exercise their own quiet leadership by raising that question ever so gently whenever circumstances warrant it. Circumstances in our Church do indeed warrant it today. Good, faithful Catholics are asking hard but helpful questions that will help us work our way through the present crisis.

We all acknowledge that authority and leadership are not the same thing. The authority conferred by sacrament and ecclesiastical systems on pastor, bishop, or pope is not now being questioned. The question is whether or not the person in authority possesses the ability to lead.

Shepherd leaders are up front and open. Transparency is not a threat to them. Service and sacrifice are their very reason for existence.

It was striking to me to read in the business press a while ago that the chairman of Arthur Andersen, Joseph Berardino, stepped down in the hope that his resignation could save his staff and their company. "Andersen Chief Says He Quit As a Sacrifice To Aid the Staff," the headline read (*New York Times*, March 28, 2002). And that, of course, related to the problems this accounting firm faced as a result of its failure to conduct an adequate audit of the Enron Corporation. Shepherd leaders are no strangers to sacrifice, but it was striking to find the term "sacrifice" in the business press, but not in the religious press reporting on our present crisis.

What we are reflecting on today, namely, the example of the Good Shepherd, has relevance for leaders in units of all sizes, for leaders in all places, seasons, and circumstances. There is something here for each one of us to apply to ourselves, to ponder over, to pray about. What kind of leader are you to those who follow you in family, classroom, store, shop, office, organization of any kind?

There is something here for us to keep in mind as we ponder and pray for our cardinals, bishops, pastors, and other Church leaders in their effort to become not just good, but better shepherds.

The Church is us—all of us. The Church is the people of God. The Church is you and I. It is saint and sinner. The Church includes the offender and the victim. The Church is more than the pope, the cardinals, bishops, priests, and religious around the world. The Church is all the laity together with their religious and priests, bishops, cardinals, and the Holy Father.

We are the Church. We are a Church in crisis. We are all in this together. We all have to respond. Consider your response today in the spirit and style of the Good Shepherd. Consider what you might do by way of prayer and fasting. Consider how you might lead, how you might be a shepherd leader, by exercising responsible followership in grateful fidelity to the Christ who called you and, as the second reading today puts it—the reading from the First Letter of Peter—"Christ also suffered for you, leaving you an example that you should follow in his footsteps." Follow you will. Lead you must. And never forget that Jesus, the Good and Eternal Shepherd, said to you, to me, to us who are the Church, "I came so that they might have life and have it more abundantly."

Pray, dear friends, that through the crisis of leadership that confronts us, the Church we love will indeed "have life and have it more abundantly."

27

Fifth Sunday of Easter

Acts 6:1–7; Psalm 33; 1 Peter 2:4–9; John 14:1–12

"WHOEVER HAS SEEN ME HAS SEEN THE FATHER"

Phillip does you a great favor by making the request you hear in today's selection from the Gospel of St. John: "Master, show us the Father."

I say Phillip is doing you a favor by making this request, because he sets the stage for a wonderful lesson from your Master Teacher. In response to the question, Jesus tells us all that anyone who sees him—observes him preaching, teaching, healing, helping—is seeing God the Father at work. Well, you may be asking, what's so special about that? Let me explain.

You believe in a Triune God—Father, Son, and Holy Spirit. The mystery of the Trinity is beyond your grasp. You accept it only on faith; you understand it incompletely at best. In other words, you could use some help in grasping the mystery of the Trinity, in coming up with a satisfactory answer to the question: What is God like?

Moreover, you worship an unseen God. You call God "Father," and so you should, but you cannot see your heavenly Father. You can see him in the effects of what he has done for you as Creator. The beauty of nature reflects the beauty of the Creator. You can see him in the goodness of those around you. The goodness of those you meet in your sojourn through life is a reflection of the goodness of God your Father. You see the effects of his divine power in the powerful forces of nature. But you can see his love—and remember, God is love—you can see his love only in love made plain for you in human form. And no one does that for you better than Jesus Christ, the Son, the divine person who is, along with the Father and the Holy Spirit, your one God.

"Master, show us the Father." And Jesus asks, with just a hint of exasperation, "Have I been with you for so long a time and you still do not know me, Philip? Whoever has seen me has seen the Father. How can you say, 'Show us the Father'? Do you not believe that I am in the Father and the Father is in me?"

Pick up on that suggestion, follow that direction. Look at the Jesus you meet in the pages of the gospel and see—when you are looking at Jesus—a reflection, not just a reminder, but a reflection of the all-powerful Father—*your* Father who is in heaven.

For example, let me take you to the road that leads out of a city called Nain. You have been there before. You found it in the seventh chapter of Luke's Gospel where you fell into step with Jesus and his disciples and a rather large crowd walking along when they came upon a small funeral procession at the city gate. The only son of a widowed mother was being carried out to burial. Luke's account tells you, "When the Lord saw her [the widowed mother] he was moved with pity for her and said to her, 'Do not weep.' He stepped forward and touched the coffin; at this the bearers halted, and he said, 'Young man, I tell you arise.' The dead man sat up and began to speak, and Jesus gave him to his mother" (Luke 7:13-15).

Now, remember, "whoever sees me, sees the Father." You see Jesus stretch out his hand and touch the stretcher that carried the dead man's body. As you look at that outstretched hand, recall the many biblical references to God's strong right arm, to the hand of God that will uphold the just and defend them from their enemies; recall the references to the hand of God in the psalms and the prophets, and then see here—as you watch Jesus—see the Father at work. See the divine pity as well as the divine power. See the Father, the heavenly Father, the all-powerful Father, moved with compassion for a poor widow. In the loving touch of Jesus see the loving touch of your Father.

Just watch Jesus, if you need help in grasping an understanding of what God your Father is like.

Other examples abound in the four Gospels. Observe Jesus talking with the Samaritan woman at the well. Listen to his conversation with the woman taken in adultery. Watch him inviting Zacchaeus to climb down from the sycamore tree and then you can follow the two of them into the home of Zacchaeus. What a house blessing that was! See Jesus feeding the five thousand. In all these compelling scenes you are seeing the Father. Why? Because, "Whoever has seen me has seen the Father." And put yourself in the place of those to whom Jesus is talking and ministering in these various events. Just a little imagination will enable you to let Jesus (and the Father) deal directly with you. Let it happen.

It is important that you apply all this to yourself. The Father is within reach—his reach of you; your reach of him. He is there—with you, around you, indeed within you. And he relates to you with compassion and pity just as Jesus reached out to encourage, heal, and befriend those he met along the way: "Whoever sees me sees the Father."

Let these thoughts sink into your soul. They are insulation against loneliness, fear, and discouragement. All your life long, you've been hearing priests and fellow believers say, "May the Lord be with you." Well it's time to convince yourself of the fact that the Lord is indeed with you—Father, Son, and Holy Spirit. And this is the same Lord who says to you, as he said to his disciples centuries ago, "I am the way, the truth, and the life." Ask for the grace today, to be able to take him at his word! If you do, you will surely know where you are going; and you will, by God's grace, be a person of peace and purpose.

28

Sixth Sunday of Easter

Acts 8:5–8, 14–17; Psalm 66; 1 Peter 3:15–18; John 14:15–21

WITH YOU ALWAYS

In this Easter season, you have your yearly reminder that there was a "doubting Thomas" among the closest followers of Jesus. Many good, struggling, want-to-be-believing people take great consolation in knowledge of that fact. They see hope for themselves in the way Jesus dealt with Thomas. He didn't scold or dismiss him. Jesus addressed Thomas's doubts and reassured him, and then encouraged him to be a believer.

All of you here today are believers. There could be, but I doubt very much that there is, a true atheist among us. Some of us might be atheists by distraction—too busy to think much about God. So confident in our own ability to draw on our own resources—our money and technological know-how—to solve any problem that might arise. We talk and act as if we were not dependent on God. We are so self-sufficient that we become, as I say, atheists by distraction. By that I mean, we don't deny that God exists, we think we don't need God! Practically speaking, we ignore God.

There is another form of creeping atheism that I've noticed in myself and others. Again, I'm not talking about classic atheism in the sense of denying the existence of God. What I have in mind is a modern, isolated, lonely, mistaken conviction that God does not exist here with me, right now, in this present moment, in my present need. Does that ring true to any of you? You're not denying that God exists; you're just not at all sure God is here with you right now.

To the extent that this is ringing any kind of a bell for you, today's readings might help.

In the second reading, the selection from the First Letter of Peter, you were reminded that "Christ also suffered for sins once, the righteous for the sake of the unrighteous, that he might lead you to God." That he might lead you—that's right, you—to God. "Put to death in the flesh, he was brought to life in the spirit."

Ponder those words. They apply to you. You, in baptism, were "put to death in the flesh." And through that same baptism, you were "brought to life in the Spirit." That's the Holy Spirit we're talking about here, and, as you know so well, the Holy Spirit is God. God brought you back to life. God dwells within you. As the saying goes, you better believe it!

And in the Gospel reading, you heard Jesus say to his original disciples and to you, "I will ask the Father, and he will give you another Advocate to be with you always." Jesus is about to leave them to return to his Father. He will not leave them orphans. He is giving them "another Advocate," another defender. And who might that be? None other than the Holy Spirit. The work and personal bodily presence of Jesus on this earth are over. But he is not abandoning his followers. He is giving them "another Advocate," another defender, another teacher, leader, guide, companion, who will be with them always.

"[H]e remains with you and will be in you," says Jesus, who speaks to you about the Holy Spirit who is now and will be always your companion, your guide, your advocate. We use the word "advocate" to describe a lawyer. We sometimes call our lawyer a "counselor." Some lawyers litigate on behalf of clients. Your lawyer is a defender who is there to represent you and protect your interests. The Holy Spirit is all of this and more to you. Your God is at your side—"with you" in the most reassuring ways—your advocate, defender, litigator, counselor. You never have to face life alone.

In today's Gospel reading, Jesus is speaking to those who love him, to men and women just like you. "If you love me," he says, "you will keep my commandments. And I will ask the Father, and he will give you another Advocate to be with you always, the Spirit of truth, whom the world cannot accept, because it neither sees nor knows him."

Well, you can't see him either, at least not directly. You can see the

Holy Spirit, however, with the eye of faith. "But you know him," Jesus says, "because he remains with you, and will be in you."

What do I want you to take away from this brief homily today, dear friends? Just that simple prepositional phrase: "with you."

He "remains with you." He "will be in you." He "will be with you always." That means today and any day next week, and every other day of your life. He is with you.

Doubt will never disqualify you from the community of believers. But don't let yourself get distracted or stuck in a "doubting Thomas" rut. Break out of it with a simple act of faith. "I believe, Lord, not simply that you exist in some abstract, distant way, but that you are here with me and for me, my Advocate, my defender, right here and now."

And to this consoling truth I invite you all to say, "Amen!"

29

Ascension

Acts 1:1–11; Psalm 47; Ephesians 1:17–23; Matthew 28:16–20

"YOU ARE TO BE MY WITNESSES"

You just heard in today's first reading the following words from the Acts of the Apostles. They were spoken by Jesus to his closest disciples just before he departed from them and ascended into heaven. These were quite literally his last words here on earth: "You will receive power when the Holy Spirit comes down on you; then you are to be my witnesses in Jerusalem, throughout Judea and Samaria, yes, even to the ends of the earth" (Acts 1:8).

"You are to be my witnesses…even to the ends of the earth." Consider those words as addressed to you—to each one of you. Hear them now centuries later, and consider them addressed to you to be acted upon now, in your own time, in your corner of the world, in the span of time that is yours. "You will receive power when the Holy Spirit comes down on you," said Jesus. Well, that time has come. The Spirit dwells within you. "Then you are to be my witnesses…even to the ends of the earth." That includes the zip code where you now live; it includes your home address, your workplace, your immediate everyday surroundings. You are to be witnesses there to the Christ who once lived here on earth, set an example of how we ordinary humans should live the good life, left us a Gospel filled with principles for positive and productive living, eventually died for us and rose again and, on the day we commemorate at this moment, ascended to heaven where he remains to this day.

And how about you? Are you sleepwalking through life or are you conscious of the fact that you are expected to be witnessing to the life, the way of life, and the words of wisdom that Jesus left behind after his ascension? As the angels said to the disciples in the account you have today from Acts, "This Jesus who has been taken from you will return, just as you saw him go up into the heavens." Well, you can only speculate on what that return might be like and when it might occur. But action, not speculation is what is expected of you now. "You are to be my witnesses," said Jesus before leaving you. How is that witnessing going? That's the question for you to consider on this celebration of the Lord's ascension. How is it going? What are you doing and saying that might help others see and understand the good news that Jesus came to bring to the world?

Love of neighbor? Assistance to the poor? Attention to the neglected? Visiting the sick? Feeding the hungry? Is there sufficient evidence on any of these fronts to convict you of giving witness to the message and ministry of Jesus? Are you keeping your commitments as he kept his? Are you praying as he instructed you to pray? Are you sharing as he hoped you would?

None of us is perfect, of course; each of us falls short of the goals we set for ourselves and most of us forget, from time to time, the high level of witnessing performance that Jesus expects of us. "You are to be my witnesses," he said. Eventually, he "will return just as you saw him go up into the heavens."

That return is unlikely to happen soon. But the witnessing to his words and works should be happening now. Quietly, effectively, persuasively, and sincerely, each one of you should be taking advantage of the opportunities that are within your reach every day to be witnesses to the life and message of Jesus. It was such a meaningful life, so attractive, so imitable. Your contemporaries can see that life played out again in your example, in the way you live your life in imitation of Christ. This is what Jesus expects of you. He is depending on you to be his hands, his eyes, his feet, his compassionate heart now that he is no longer walking the earth. To the extent that you make him visible—that you witness to his ways, and words, and works—he will be seen by your contemporaries who, accordingly, can be drawn to believe in and follow him.

This witness ministry never ends. You are capable of participating in it as long as you have breath. At no stage of life, however old, immobile, or dependent you become, are you unable to witness to the patient self-donation that was the life of Jesus here on earth. You surely do not need a reminder from me to indicate how great the need is today here on earth to have more of the loving presence of Jesus in our midst.

Even though he has ascended into heaven, you are still here on earth. He is depending on you to bear witness to him. Pray today for the grace to be up to the challenge!

30

Seventh Sunday of Easter

Acts 1:12–14; Psalm 27; 1 Peter 4:13–16; John 17:1–11

"NOW THIS IS ETERNAL LIFE"

Today's Gospel reading begins with an early verse in John 17. For centuries now, this selection has been known as the "high priestly prayer" of Jesus. I want to focus your attention on one sentence—a sentence, by the way, that was surely edited into the text in the early years of the life of the Church. Here it is: "Now this is eternal life, that they should know you, the only true God, and the one whom you sent, Jesus Christ." I say it was edited in, or added by those who assembled the sayings of Jesus from the oral tradition and eventually put them into written form, because Jesus never referred to himself by name—Jesus Christ—anywhere else in the Gospels.

In any case, this is from a prayer put on the lips of Jesus, a prayer addressed directly to God the Father. And this is now part of the inspired word of God that we have in our canonical Scriptures. In this prayer Jesus makes intercession for those present around him just before his ascension, namely, his disciples, who can hear him—overhear him, so to speak—as he prays to the Father. And he makes intercession also in this high-priestly prayer for future generations of disciples, for you and for me.

Reflect with me, therefore, for a few moments now on the meaning of the prayer he made for you: that you may have eternal life. And then explore with me the description he gives of eternal life. "Now this is eternal life," says Jesus, speaking to the Father in the hearing of his disciples, to "know you, the only true God, and him whom you have sent."

What's it going to be like in heaven? What will happen there? What is heaven all about? The simple, but also profound, answer to that question is this: knowledge. Not knowledge of the book-learning variety, not knowledge as the end of a long and perhaps brain-fatiguing search. But knowledge of the person of the Father, of him whom the Father sent; knowledge of oneself, of those you have loved here on earth; knowledge of all things good and beautiful; knowledge of truth in all its forms. That's what heaven is all about.

A hymn that is part of Night Prayer in the Liturgy of the Hours (the Divine Office or "Breviary," as it is sometimes called) says it nicely, "We praise you, Father, for your gifts/ Of dusk and nightfall over earth, / Foreshadowing the mystery / of death that leads to *endless day*."

Endless day—that is a good way of describing heaven. Once you get there, you are eternally awake and eternally aware. The English word "enthusiasm" comes from two Greek words, *en theos* meaning, "in God." And that is what those who are in heaven experience forever. We can only speculate on what eternal enthusiasm is like for them.

They know the generations that have gone before them. They know them all. They know the saints to whom they prayed, the historical figures they admired, the billions of others whom they knew existed, but never knew personally. And they are reunited with those they loved when they shared space and life with them here on this earth. They are all now part of this eternal awareness. All the mysteries of faith are part of that awareness; they are mysteries no longer. And the "mysteries" of things humanistic and scientific that any given mind may not have managed to translate from print to mental assimilation here on earth, they are known in eternal life; they are mysteries no longer.

Endless day. Endless awareness, endless enthusiasm—*en theos*—in God; knowledge to the full.

"Now this is eternal life, that they should know you, the only true God, and him whom you sent, Jesus Christ." You will literally "know it all;" and knowledge will be yours without a hint of pride, an echo of arrogance, or a shade of superiority. It will be yours with deep gratitude, high praise, and abiding joy.

That's what heaven is all about. Get yourself ready for it now. And in anticipation, add an expectant "Amen" to these words of St. Paul, found in the First Letter to the Corinthians, namely that "Eye has not seen, and ear has not heard, [nor has it] entered the human heart what God has prepared for those who love him" (2:9).

There it is, waiting for you.

31

Vigil of Pentecost

Genesis 11:1–9 (or others); Psalm 104; Romans 8:22–27;
John 7:37–39

"IN HOPE WE WERE SAVED"

On this, the Vigil of Pentecost we celebrate, in an anticipatory way, with faith-filled hearts the coming of the Holy Spirit. The second reading, a selection from Paul's Letter to the Romans (8:22–27) reminds us that "[i]n hope we were saved." And Paul goes on to offer the instruction that "hoping for what we cannot see means awaiting it with patient endurance."

Give some thought, therefore, on this Vigil of Pentecost to the idea of hope, and remind yourself of the wisdom of waiting for what you hope for with "patient endurance." Each one of us is hoping to be united with God for all eternity in heaven. We are hopeful. We have reason to be hopeful because of the gift each one of us received in the person of the Holy Spirit who dwells within us.

Now you have to consider carefully the words St. Paul uses in this selection you have today from Romans in order to understand what it is that the Holy Spirit is doing—or, better, wants to do if we will only cooperate—within us. St. Paul says: "The Spirit too helps us in our weakness for we do not know how to pray as we ought; but the Spirit himself makes intercession for us with groanings which cannot be expressed in speech."

We do not know how to pray. The Spirit does. The Holy Spirit of God is there waiting and willing to pray within you, to let what Paul calls "groanings" rise from within you to reach the ear of God. As Paul indicates, God "who searches hearts knows what the Spirit means [in these "groanings"], for the Spirit intercedes for the saints [that's Paul's reference to you] as God himself wills."

Try to unpack all of that to get at the lesson Paul is giving you today. You will surely acknowledge that you don't know all there is to know about prayer and that you can use some help. You can therefore be grateful that, according to Paul, help has already come in the person and presence of the Holy Spirit. Your own familiar groanings of fatigue and discouragement, as you work your way through life trying to figure things out, should not be permitted to drown out the inspired "groanings" that are now rising from within you in the utterances of the Holy Spirit. Listen for them. Try to figure them out. Let them nudge you in a Godward direction. They will surely include expressions of praise for God. They will also include expressions of thanks from you to God for God's saving work on your behalf. Probably they will include requests for direction from God, for divine guidance as you approach decision points in your life, for divine inspiration relating to what God expects you to be doing with the time and talent that are yours. Just listening prayerfully to the questions embodied in those "groanings" may enable you to discover the answers. Remember, it is the Spirit groaning within you.

Your mood on this Vigil of Pentecost should be quiet and anticipatory. Your attitude, as I suggested earlier, should be hopeful. It might be both comforting and somewhat reassuring for you to recall that G. K. Chesterton once remarked that hope is no virtue at all unless things are really hopeless! The more hopeless things appear in your life, the more reason you have to turn in hope to God and rely on the indwelling Spirit.

The Universal Church is praying with you today in the words of the Alleluia verse proclaimed before the reading of the Gospel: "Come, Holy Spirit, fill the hearts of your faithful; and kindle in them the fire of your love." That's your prayer for yourself on this Vigil of Pentecost; that's your prayer for all your brothers and sisters in the community of faith. What a wonderful thing it would be we could all move forward today, quite literally "fired up" with the presence, power, and love of the Holy Spirit within us. We could surely then expect to see, by God's grace, some evidence in this our day of renewal on the face of the earth!

What a wonderful payoff that would be for the "patient endurance" St. Paul asked each of you to have.

32

Pentecost Sunday

Acts 2:1–11; Psalm 104; 1 Corinthians 12:3b–7, 12–13;
John 14:15–16, 23b–26

A PENTECOST REFLECTION: WHAT IS GOD LIKE?

There are really only two basic or fundamental theological questions:
What is God like? And how must I act, what must I do to please God?
Or, to put that second question another way: what must I do to do the
right thing? We tend to become so preoccupied with the second question that we fail to appreciate the importance of the first.

What is God like? Let that question carry you into a prayerful mood
this morning, a reflective mode, and let yourself enjoy a prayerful pondering into the mystery beyond all other mysteries, the mystery of God
who revealed himself to us in the person of Jesus Christ.

They tell a story about Jesuit Cardinal Avery Dulles, the great theologian, who once addressed a religious assembly from a podium that
had a banner on the wall behind it that read, "God Is Other People."
As he stepped up to the podium, Avery Dulles ran his theological eye
across that line and then turned to the audience and said, "The way
that sign should really read, is: 'God is other, people!'"

Indeed God is other—altogether and totally other. But, as any theologian would assure you, you can take a faith-based journey of exploration into God through prayer and also through theological reflection.
St. Thomas Aquinas, borrowing from St. Anselm, said that theology is
fides quaerens intellectum, faith seeking understanding. You can seek
to understand God, and your seeking through prayer or study will be
rewarded with some greater insight, some more understanding of the
inexhaustible mystery that is our God.

What is God like?

Well, let's take another look at today's readings from Scripture. But before we do, let's recall that God is Triune—three Divine Persons in one God, in one Divine Nature: Father, Son, and Holy Spirit. Theology encourages us to think of the Father as Creator, the Son as Redeemer, and the Holy Spirit as Sanctifier, although we know that all three Divine Persons create, redeem, and sanctify.

It is easy to think of God as Father; everyone knows what a good father is like. It is also easy to think of God as Son; everyone is familiar with the idea of sonship. But God the Holy Spirit? It is not as easy to picture that or to grasp the idea. Spirit implies immateriality and invisibility. Literally and figuratively, it is hard to picture the Holy Spirit as we ponder the question: What is God like? It is at this point that today's Scripture can be helpful.

In the First Reading, a selection from the Acts of the Apostles, you heard the words: "When the time for Pentecost was fulfilled, they were all in one place together. And suddenly there came from the sky a noise like a strong driving wind, and it filled the entire house in which they were. Then there appeared to them tongues as of fire, which parted and came to rest on each one of them. And they were all filled with the Holy Spirit..." What is God the Holy Spirit like? Like a wind, like a flame. Like a strong wind or a gentle breeze, the Spirit can be present to you. Like fire, the Spirit can bring you light and warmth. "Come, Holy Spirit, fill the hearts of the faithful and kindle in them the fire of your love."

What is God like? God is like a breeze. God is like a flickering flame. God is like love—seen with the inner eye, felt in the heart.

And in the reading from First Corinthians you were reminded that "There are different kinds of spiritual gifts but the same Spirit"; "and we were all given to drink of one Spirit." God the Holy Spirit is a spirit of unity. We can drink in—imbibe—the Holy Spirit and become refreshed, recommitted, rededicated.

In John 14, there is a reference to the Spirit as lawyer. "And I will ask the Father, and he will give you another Advocate to be with you always." Your advocate, your lawyer, your defender, your promoter of right relationships is the Holy Spirit. And the Spirit is also your teacher. "I have told you this while I am with you," Jesus said to his closest friends, "The Advocate, the Holy Spirit whom the Father will send in my name, will teach you everything and remind you of all that I told you."

So, what is God like? Like a great father. Like a wonderful son. Like a wind in your sail, a warming and enlightening flame in your heart. Like an advocate, a special pleader, for you. Like a teacher who will instruct you if you only calm down and open up your heart to listen.

And the Holy Spirit, whose coming upon us we celebrate on this day, Pentecost Sunday, the Holy Spirit brings gifts: wisdom, understanding, knowledge, counsel (or right judgment), fortitude (which is the courage all of us need), piety (understood as a mature and proper reverence), and the last on this list of gifts is what is called "fear of the Lord," meaning a certain sense of wonder and awe. These are the gifts of Pentecost, the gifts we celebrate today. These gifts enable us to work along with God in our own day for the salvation of our world. These gifts are the outpouring of God's love and the Holy Spirit is the mystery of God's love in our world.

What is God like? Ultimately, God is love. And all these qualities, ideas, and images we've been considering add up to that one word. For God is love and we celebrate God's gift of love to us on this Pentecost Sunday.

VI
Ordinary Time

. . . .

33

Second Sunday of the Year

Isaiah 49:3, 5–6; Psalm 40; 1 Corinthians 1:1–3; John 1:29–34

"HERE AM I, LORD; I COME TO DO YOUR WILL"

Here we are, dear friends, back in what the Church calls "Ordinary Time." We've made it through Lent; we've celebrated Easter and ascension; we've been fired with enthusiasm by recalling the Pentecost experience; and now it is back to "ordinary" time. This means back to the day-by-day following of Christ, to the daily search for the will of God, to the prayerful and sacramental expression of praise and thanks to God for the salvation that is ours through Christ Jesus, and to the service of one another as we try to live out the commandment of love that Jesus gave us.

We don't have to be heroic; we just have to be faithful, leading ordinary lives in Ordinary Time. We are all busy about many things. God expects us to be caught up in the care of family, the task of building a better world through our secular pursuits, the development of our potential for becoming more completely human. We are expected to be busy about many things. Or we may be slowing down. We may be aging; we may be ill. Nevertheless, we are alive by the grace of God. Underlying it all, at every stage of life, is our quest for the will of God.

Ordinary Time brings us back to ordinary readings from Scripture—some not so familiar readings from the Old Testament, many much more familiar selections from the letters of Paul, and weekly visits with one of the evangelists, Matthew, Mark, Luke, or John. Jesus is present there in the word. He becomes more present to us as we hear the word of God and let it penetrate our consciousness.

Now I want to lift a few words from the Responsorial Psalm in today's liturgy. As you know, the first reading, always from the Old

Testament, is followed by a response each week from the Book of Psalms. The psalms are recited or sung throughout the world in the Divine Office each day. Monks and nuns sing them in their monasteries; priests read them throughout the day by picking up the Breviary. (Some do that while walking and call it "pushing the book.") Laypersons too turn to the psalms each day. The Psalter can serve as a prayer book for any believer. The psalmist knew the human condition and understood human feelings. The psalms wrap words around the unexpressed thoughts that roil the emotions of persons in distress. They also provide phrases suitable for prayer from tranquil hearts desiring to draw closer to God.

The words I want to lift for your consideration from today's Responsorial Psalm, Psalm 40, are these: "Here am I, Lord; I come to do your will." They touch upon the central challenge of your life, namely, the discovery of God's will for you and your response to that will. They touch upon your readiness to align your free will with the will of God. There is, of course, a broad direction for your life that God wills you to follow. Most of you know what that is and are comfortable with your movement in that direction. There is also God's will for you in the particulars on life—making this choice or that, helping here or repairing there, taking this or giving that.

You should realize that Scripture is a "two-edged sword" (Heb 4:12). You can hear the inspired words as God's voice speaking to you, saying, for example, "take courage; be stout-hearted" (Ps 27), and they can be used as your words spoken to God, as I'm suggesting in this instance today: "Here am I, Lord; I come to do your will."

Speaking specifically of the psalms, the late Carmelite scholar Roland Murphy acknowledged their universal appeal and practical utility for any believer: "For in these prayers," he wrote, "is expressed the basic reactions of (the human person) before God—faith, joy, fear, trust, and praise—language that no one can fail to understand."

It is a mistake for you to think of God's will in a fatalistic way, as if you have no freedom or responsibility in the face of the divine will. You do indeed have freedom and you are responsible for using that freedom well and wisely, hence the importance for you of setting your compass in alignment with the will of God for you. You can't do that unless you seek out the will of God—unless you declare yourself to be ready and willing ("Here am I, Lord; I come to do your will") and really mean it.

It begins with you listening. You can listen to Scripture, and you should. You should not read the Bible as if it were a novel or a textbook; you should simply open it from time to time and listen to what you see on the printed page! For many believers, the favorite place to open the Bible for these prayerful listening sessions is the Book of Psalms.

It's been said that without faith, Scripture is an unlighted torch. So bring your faith to the Book! It has also been said, "When we read inspired texts, we go to school with the Holy Spirit." So return to school and recognize the Spirit as your tutor when you pick up the Book of Psalms.

Speak to God from your heart in the words we've lifted today from Psalm 40: "Here am I, Lord; I come to do your will." Wait for the Lord's response. Is there restlessness now in your life, a sense that you should be moving on to something else, or trying something new? Is there an anxiety in your life through which the Lord might be speaking to you? Try listening through your gut. By that, I mean, read your feelings carefully because God might be communicating to you through your feelings. Because they are feelings, you cannot escape them. They are there. They just might be saying something to you that God wants you to hear. Don't turn them off. Don't shut down this communications system. Listen to God and have the courage to respond.

"Here am I, Lord; I come to do your will." Don't be surprised if God makes his will known to you through your inclinations toward something new and positive. Let yourself think, even say aloud, "I feel I should be doing this or that; I feel the time is right." That feeling may be from God. That feeling may be reinforced by other words and phrases that you will find in the psalms. You can turn to your feelings for confirmation of the new direction you might now be inspired to take. Take it, and see how it feels. If the feeling is one of peace and a sense of "that's right for me," you'll know that your will is aligned with the will of God for you.

You're on your way into Ordinary Time!

34

Third Sunday of the Year

Isaiah 8:23—9:3; Psalm 27; 1 Corinthians 1:10–13, 17;
Matthew 4:12–17

THE PRIEST SHORTAGE

Walk along this morning with Jesus by the Sea of Galilee, where you find him in today's Gospel account. He sees Simon Peter and Simon's brother Andrew. They are fishermen and, as Jesus walks by, they are casting their nets into the sea. And Jesus said to them, "Come after me, and I will make you fishers of men." This is a call to discipleship. This is a call to all men and women in all stages of life—"Come," he says to every believer—to you and me today—"come and walk along with me," says Jesus, "come follow me."

Let's pause here with Jesus, Peter, and Andrew, and open our eyes to the scene and our ears to the words. Then, taking the opportunity occasioned by this particular passage in Matthew's Gospel, let's try as best we can to open our minds to the question of the status and supply of priests in the Church in the United States today. The call that we hear in this morning's Gospel is not explicitly or exclusively a call to ordained priesthood. It is a call to discipleship. However, some disciples are called to priesthood and it is to that call, the call to priesthood, that I would direct your attention for a few moments now.

Dean Hoge, the late sociologist of religion who taught at The Catholic University of America, was a Presbyterian who for about twenty years studied what he typically referred to as "the priest shortage" in the American Catholic Church. Not everyone would agree, despite the clear evidence of declining numbers, that there is a shortage of priests in the United States; some would say there is just a shortage of celebrants! Others would argue that God wills this to be a new age of opportunity for lay ministry; fewer clergy are needed. Or they will assert that if the Catholic Church ordained women, or admitted married men to holy orders, there would be more than enough ordained pastors to tend to the needs of the flock.

Say what you think about this situation as you walk along at this hour with Jesus, Peter, and Andrew; at least say it to yourself. Try to imagine what they—Jesus, Andrew, and Peter—might want to say to you by way of comment on our priest shortage in America today. Be open to the possibility that Christ might be calling you, or expecting you to encourage others to be open to the call to priesthood.

We Jesuits of the Maryland Province went through a Province-wide consultation process some years ago as we considered our needs and who might best lead us for the next six years as Fr. Tim Brown, of Loyola College (now University) in Baltimore, was selected to be our next Provincial. The need to increase our Jesuit ranks with more vocations was seen to be the most pressing need we faced at that time. So, to the extent that we as a Province might weigh in on the consideration I'm inviting you to entertain for a few minutes now, we Jesuits would say, yes, there is a priest shortage, and, yes, we hope Christ will tap on the shoulder some modern Peters and Andrews, and invite them to drop their nets (Internets or any other kind) and free themselves up to follow him, to answer in the affirmative when he says, "Come after me, and I will make you fishers of men."

Some of you might wince at the phrase, "fishers of men." I feel certain that if Jesus were here among us at the moment, he would surely say "fishers of men and women," fishers or servants of all humankind. And here with us in a modern technological society, he would be looking for generous and competent Peters and Andrews in a world not limited to fishing nets, but a modern world of telecommunications and broadcast networks, a commercial world of supply networks, a scientific world of information networks, a world of political networks, an interdependent, interconnected world of human beings all in need of salvation in and through the redemptive sacrifice of Christ. And Christ, as you know, chooses to work the salvation of the world though the ministry of his disciples, humans like you and me, some of whom he wants to serve as priests.

Are the Andreas and Petras of our modern Catholic community not included in this call? All—men and women alike—are called to discipleship, to follow Christ. But are the Andreas and Petras excluded from the call to ordained priestly ministry in our Church today? Yes they are now. Will that last forever? Who can say? Surely, no one can say with certainty that they will never be called to priesthood since, as we all know, "nothing is impossible with God" (Luke 1:37). But not for now.

Nor are married men now called to ordination in our Church although that may change in the nearer term. For now, however, we know that our Church admits to the ranks of the ordained only men committed to celibacy. What might Jesus, Andrew, and Peter be saying to you about that as you walk along in conversation today?

I don't know what they are saying to you. Like you, I can speculate on what they might be saying, but I don't know for sure. I do know this, however—Andrew and Peter, two of the pillars on which our Church was founded, would surely want to see the priesthood continue on in service to the human community in our modern times. If this is to happen, the Church needs priests. And I feel certain that Peter and Andrew, and Christ himself, would urge patience on us all as Christ invites some few to give themselves in freedom to ordained ministry in and for the people of God.

Dean Hoge would surely tell us, if he were here today, that his research shows celibacy to be a major obstacle encountered by young men when they face up to the question of whether or not priesthood is their calling. Lifetime commitment is another obstacle. So is the exclusion of women from orders. Anyone who surveys the young to get at their thinking on this issue will agree that these three are major obstacles. These are institutional barriers, if you will, matters that have to be attended to—not necessarily changed, but given careful consideration—by a listening, reflective Church that is obedient to the will of God.

Meanwhile, you and I, men and women, young and old (but young men in particular) have to give this question the attention it deserves (as Andrew and Peter were attentive to this vocational issue, and responsive, when they heard Jesus say, "Come after me.").

Give some thought to the symbolic meaning of our standing to hear the Gospel proclaimed at Mass each Sunday. Why do we stand to hear the proclamation of the Gospel? Our standing symbolizes our readiness to respond, to move in whatever direction the Gospel message urges us to move. In the context of today's Gospel, and in the face of a priest shortage in the United States today, I would hope that you would be ready, first to pray to God to call more young men to priesthood, and, if you happen to be a young man, to pray that you might be ready to take the necessary steps, if that is what God is asking of you, that will lead to the form of discipleship that is ordained priesthood.

Jesus said to Peter and Andrew, "'Come after me, and I will make you fishers of men. At once they left their nets and followed him. He walked along from there and saw two other brothers, James, the son of Zebedee, and his brother John. They were in a boat, with their father Zebedee, mending their nets. He called them, and immediately they left their boat and their father and followed him. He went around all of Galilee, teaching in their synagogues, proclaiming the gospel of the kingdom, and curing every disease and illness among the people."

They followed him. And there, dear friends, lies the lesson for us all. And note that he invited them to become part of a movement; he had no construction plans for the building of a monument! That's another lesson to consider now.

35

Fourth Sunday of the Year

Zephaniah 2:3; 3:12–13; Psalm 146; 1 Corinthians 1:26–31;
Matthew 5:1–12

"NOT MANY OF YOU ARE WISE…; NOT MANY ARE WELL-BORN" (THE BEATITUDES)

Let me invite you to return for a moment to the second reading, the selection you heard from Paul's First Letter to the Corinthians, before we consider together the famous and familiar verses from the Sermon on the Mount that constitute what we call "The Beatitudes."

The second reading is not all that flattering to you. "Brothers and Sisters," says St. Paul, "Consider your own situation. Not many of you were wise…; not many were powerful; not many were of noble birth. Rather, God chose the foolish of the world to shame the wise, and God chose the weak of the world to shame the strong." That's you—not wise, not influential, not well-born. He even notes that you are among those "who count for nothing."

Well, at least you can take some consolation in knowing that you are chosen! But there is no room for complacency here. Like it or not, you are, by God's holy will, countercultural. Your values are not this world's values. What you prize is not (or, at least should not be) what the world holds dear. And today's liturgy offers you this humbling reminder from St. Paul in order to prepare you to hear, possibly for the first time, the countercultural message of the beatitudes.

In the fifth chapter of Matthew's Gospel, as you just heard, there is this account of the teaching Jesus presenting a concise summary of what it means to be a Christian, even though at that point in history there were no Christians. Nor was there a Catholic Church. But the following set of ideas, intended to both describe and define Catholic

Christians, was there for all within the range of the voice of Christ to consider those many centuries ago:

> When he saw the crowds, he went up the mountain, and after he had sat down, his disciples came to him. He began to teach them, saying:
>
> "Blessed are the poor in spirit,
> for theirs is the kingdom of heaven.
> Blessed are they who mourn, for they will be comforted.
> Blessed are the meek, for they will inherit the land.
> Blessed are they who hunger and thirst for righteousness,
> for they will be satisfied.
> Blessed are the merciful, for they will be shown mercy.
> Blessed are the clean of heart, for they will see God.
> Blessed are the peacemakers, for they will be called children
> of God.
> Blessed are they who are persecuted for the sake of
> righteousness, for theirs is the kingdom of heaven.
> Blessed are you when they insult you and persecute you and
> utter every kind of evil against you [falsely] because of me.
> Rejoice and be glad, for your reward will be great in heaven.
> Thus they persecuted the prophets who were before you."

These are the so-called "Beatitudes"—happiness qualities, blessings, although it takes faith to see the happiness there, to welcome them as blessings in your life. There are eight categories: (1) the poor in spirit, (2) those who mourn, (3) the meek, (4) those who hunger and thirst for justice, (5) the merciful, (6) the clean-hearted, (7) the peacemakers, and (8) the persecuted.

A somewhat different version appears in the sixth chapter of the Gospel of Luke, a bit shorter and even more countercultural than Matthew's list. In Luke you read:

> And he came down with them and stood on a stretch of level ground. A great crowd of his disciples and a large number of the

people from all Judea and Jerusalem and the coastal region of Tyre and Sidon came to hear him and to be healed of their diseases; and even those who were tormented by unclean spirits were cured.

Everyone in the crowd sought to touch him because power came forth from him and healed them all.

And raising his eyes toward his disciples he said: "Blessed are you who are poor, for the kingdom of God is yours.

Blessed are you who are now hungry, for you will be satisfied. Blessed are you who are now weeping, for you will laugh.

Blessed are you when people hate you, and when they exclude and insult you, and denounce your name as evil on account of the Son of Man.

Rejoice and leap for joy on that day! Behold, your reward will be great in heaven. For their ancestors treated the prophets in the same way." (vv. 17–23)

The words that emerge here speak simply and starkly of the poor, the hungry, the weeping, the hated, excluded, and insulted. Note that Luke says poor, not poor in spirit.

During election campaigns in the United States, there is often discussion about how Catholics should vote and how presidential candidates and other office seekers match up against Catholic teaching, values, principles, and ideals. When those questions arise, I say hold up the candidates and their party platforms against the background of the Beatitudes in order to see how well they match up. There is no perfect match, of course, but this doesn't mean that the exercise is futile. It serves to remind that the core message of Christianity is summarized in the Beatitudes.

Put yourself at this moment in that crowd you just saw in the Gospel. Fix your eyes on Christ. Listen intently.

"He began to teach them, saying: Blessed are the poor in spirit." Jesus was teaching a healthy detachment here; urging those who would follow him not to be possessed by their possessions; to fix their hearts on higher things and not to get caught in the trappings of wealth.

"Blessed are they who mourn." Mourning is part of life, as we all know. But so is the comfort that only God can give and that only the faithful heart can know.

"Blessed are the meek." Meekness is not weakness; never confuse timidity with humility. True humility is courage. Christian meekness is uncommon courage, the courage of the cross.

"Blessed are they who hunger and thirst for justice." Justice is fairness. It involves the protection and promotion of just relationships. It is truly God's work.

"Blessed are the merciful, for they will be shown mercy." Firm, but gentle; shrewd, but ever forgiving; that's the way you temper justice with mercy, in imitation of the just man who first articulated these Beatitudes.

"Blessed are the clean of heart, for they will see God." This Beatitude praises the pure-hearted, the person of integrity, and it delivers a promise that all of us hope for—to see God, as Jesus promised we would, if only we are just. That's the reward of pure-heartedness, of being clean and clear of heart, of being the polar opposite of the double-minded person.

"Blessed are the peacemakers." We all have to be reconcilers, dispute resolvers, mediators. All of us are called to contribute to the cause of peace. If we do, peace will be ours forever.

"Blessed are they who are persecuted for the sake of justice, for theirs is the kingdom of heaven." To some extent, this can and will happen to all of us. No one can go through life without encountering some misunderstanding, unfair treatment, under-appreciation, and occasional recrimination. That's what it means to be a disciple, a follower, an imitator of Christ.

"Blessed are you when they insult you and persecute you and utter every kind of evil against you [falsely] because of me." To the extent that any of this comes your way in the line of duty, so to speak, on the path of Christian discipleship, so much the loss for the persecutors and so much the gain, the eternal gain, for you.

"Rejoice and be glad, for your reward will be great in heaven." And that, my friends, says it all!

St. Leo the Great was a pope who died in the year 461. He once gave a sermon on the Beatitudes in which he said, "When our Lord Jesus Christ was preaching the Gospel of the kingdom and healing various illnesses throughout the whole of Galilee, the fame of his mighty works spread into all of Syria, and great crowds from all parts of Judea flocked to the heavenly physician." And then Leo pointed out that those who were to be instructed in the divine message "had first to be aroused by bodily benefits and visible miracles so that, once they had experienced his gracious power, they would no longer doubt his doctrine."

In other words, Pope Leo is saying that the miracles Jesus performed got the people's attention, but "in order to cure men's souls now that he had healed their bodies, Our Lord climbed to the solitude of a neighboring mountain, and called the apostles to himself."

Leo suggests a parallel between this mountain for the so-called Sermon on the Mount, and Mount Sinai where the Lord met Moses and gave him the Ten Commandments. The message to Moses, said Pope Leo, "evidenced a terrifying justice." But the words we are considering now in the Sermon of Jesus on the Mount, "reveal a sacred compassion." It is, says Leo, a "tranquil discourse." Listen again to Leo the Great: "Concerning the content of Christ's teaching, his own sacred words bear witness; thus whoever longs to attain eternal blessedness can now recognize the steps that lead to that high happiness."

The steps, of course, are the eight Beatitudes. They lead you home to heaven.

36

Fifth Sunday of the Year

Isaiah 58:7–10; Psalm 112; 1 Corinthians 2:1–5; Matthew 5:13–16

"YOU ARE THE SALT OF THE EARTH; YOU ARE THE LIGHT OF THE WORLD"

Take the compliments while you can! You just heard Jesus say to you in this Gospel reading: "You are the salt of the earth; you are the light of the world." Nice compliments. Not deserved? That's okay; take them anyway as ideals to live up to, as goals to be sought out in the months and years ahead.

When you listen to the Gospels you can believe that Jesus speaks through his disciples to you, who are his contemporary disciples, the only ones he has alive and kicking on this corner of the earth, in this moment in time. There he is and here you are. He is speaking to you. Try to listen. There is, of course, a gap between you; there is a significant spread of years. You are literally centuries apart. There may even be something of a cultural gap between you. He was quite literally a man of another age. You have to be careful that you understand what he says, and that you really are hearing his words.

So it might be worth taking a few moments to settle on the meaning of the expressions he used—"salt of the earth" and "light of the world"—so that you cannot just enjoy the compliment but so that you can take it to heart and let it work from within your heart as a driver of your dreams.

What might Jesus have meant by "salt of the earth?" That's an expression, as you know, that has survived down through the centuries; it is often employed in a complimentary way in referring to a genuinely fine person. Salt has always been used as a seasoning and a preservative. It is a necessity for life and good health. In the time of Jesus, the word was used metaphorically in reference to loyalty, durability, and fidelity. So to be called "salt of the earth" was a tribute to your integrity as a person. Salt was also used as a unit of exchange. You may have heard the expression—"he's worth his salt"—meaning worthy of his pay. In any case, to be thought of as "the salt of the earth" is to be held in very high regard.

But "what if salt goes flat?" as Jesus asks in this Gospel story; what if the salt "loses its flavor"? "Then it is good for nothing but to be thrown out and trampled underfoot." This is a warning against infidelity, against abandoning the good news. If the disciple loses the message, then discipleship itself will be lost. So, in accepting the compliment that Jesus offers you today when he says, "You are the salt of the earth," renew your commitment to him and to his message. Make sure you preserve that message. And, as is so often the case with religious realities, you keep good things by giving them away. So in recommitting yourself today to Christ and his message, recommit yourself to the evangelical task of spreading that word, of sharing the good news with others.

As you do, you can quite literally become "the light of the world," the second compliment paid to you in today's Gospel. "You are the light of the world. A city set on a mountain cannot be hidden," says Jesus. "Nor do they light a lamp and then put it under a bushel basket; it is set on a lampstand where it gives light to all in the house. Just so, your light must shine before others, that they may see your good deeds and glorify your heavenly Father."

These are dark days and Jesus is asking you to brighten them up. He is urging you to show forth—not show off, but show forth—your good works. No braggadocio here, just straightforward good example. No false humility, just stand-up, let-the-whole-world-see some good example—your good example. These are indeed dark days—in the Church and in the world. There is darkness in the suffering and poverty of many. There is darkness is the deceit and hypocrisy of many should-be leaders. There is darkness in scandal and crime. There is darkness in terrorist threats. There is darkness in the fears that envelop so many people. What they need to see is the light and they can see the light in the good works that you do, in your generous deeds, in your standing up and speaking out, in your open hands and warm embrace.

Just be a genuinely good person—the salt of the earth—and don't succumb to a false humility that would have you hide your goodness under a bushel basket. The world needs a few more smiles, a few more pats on the back, a few more acts of generosity, a few more thoughtful notes and unexpected telephone calls. The world needs more virtue, of course, more truth telling and caregiving. You've got plenty to give, so go ahead and give! And don't worry about people noticing what you do. Let them notice. Not so that they can admire you, but so, as Jesus said, "they may glorify your heavenly Father."

37

Sixth Sunday of the Year

Sirach 15:15–20; Psalm 119; 1 Corinthians 2:6–10; Matthew 5:17–37

THE HIGHER STANDARD: SURPASSING THE SCRIBES AND THE PHARISEES

Today's Gospel sets a higher standard for all of you. Jesus reminds you that if you want to enter the kingdom of God, you're going to have to do better than the scribes and Pharisees. They, as you know, are sticklers to the law, preoccupied with minutiae and endless details. Well, Jesus brushes that kind of fundamentalism aside in his message to you today and, far from encouraging you to ignore the law, proceeds to set a higher moral standard for you—for all of us who would be his followers.

There is something of a rhythm in his remarks here: "You have heard that it was said…. But I say to you…" He repeats this rhythm several times. Listen to these three assertions made by Jesus, each raises the moral standard, setting the bar higher for those who would follow him.

"You have heard that it was said to your ancestors, 'You shall not kill; and whoever kills will be liable to judgment.' But *I say to you*: whoever is angry with his brother will be liable to judgment." Avoiding murder is not sufficient; you've got to avoid anger. The higher standard.

"You have heard that it was said, 'You shall not commit adultery.' *But I say to you*: everyone who looks at a woman with lust has already committed adultery with her in his heart." Again, the higher standard. The act of adultery is clearly prohibited, but so is the lustful look, the unworthy and secret desire. There again, the higher standard.

"Again you have heard that it was said to your ancestors, 'Do not take a false oath, but make good to the Lord all that you vow. *But I say to you*, do not swear at all. Let your 'Yes' mean 'Yes" and your 'No' mean 'No.' Anything more is from the evil one." And there again, you have the higher standard. Not only may you not lie or swear falsely, you should not swear at all. You should be forthright, straightforward, direct, and completely honest. For you, "Yes" should always mean "Yes" and "No" always mean "No." There is no evasion, no waffling, no wiggling through the loopholes for those who would follow Christ.

Let's take these three goals—avoiding anger, abolishing lustful desire, and committing oneself to honest speech—and consider not only how much our personal morality would improve if we adopted them as personal objectives, but also how much better off our world would be if all its inhabitants made these goals their own. The commitment to anger avoidance would mean non-violence in our midst and hence an end to war. The commitment to purity of heart would mean an end to pornography, prostitution, sexual exploitation, and marital infidelity. The commitment to truth-telling would mean integrity in business, government, and all other areas of human interaction. What a social revolution that would be! What a better world we would have!

When you think about it, Jesus was really a social revolutionary. He wanted to turn things around. His, of course, would be a completely non-violent revolution. It involves a turnaround in the minds and hearts of us humans. He created all who inhabit the world. He created them out of love for them. He wants nothing but their happiness and eternal security. And he laid out the path for achieving happiness and security by the teaching and example of his own life. Here in today's Gospel you have some of his teaching. He is showing you the way. His instruction is non-threatening and non-coercive. It is all pretty simple. He lays it out clearly for your consideration. He awaits your free response. Don't keep him waiting.

He knows that he has set a higher standard for you than was the case, as he puts it, for your "ancestors." But they didn't have the example of Jesus, as you have, or the teaching of his Church, or the help of his sacraments, as you have. Sure, the standard is high and you will not always achieve it or, when achieved, maintain it. But you've got to stretch, to reach, to keep on trying.

This is not a Sisyphean struggle. You won't find it discouraging because the more you persist in your attempt to make progress toward these three goals, the more pleasant life around you will become. There will be less friction, turmoil, hurt, misunderstanding, and complication. That's the way it should be with life on the way to kingdom. And that indeed is the life to which each one of you is called.

That's why you can apply to yourself the words of today's Responsorial Psalm: "Blessed are they who follow the law of the Lord!" (Ps 119:1). Be happy and high-hearted as you continue on your way!

38

Seventh Sunday of the Year

Leviticus 19:1–2, 17–18; Psalm 103; 1 Corinthians 3:16–23;
Matthew 5:38–48

TEMPLE OF THE HOLY SPIRIT

"Do you not know that you are the temple of God, and that the Spirit of God dwells in you? If anyone destroys God's temple, God will destroy that person; for the temple of God, which you are, is holy." (1 Cor 3:16–17)

Those are remarkable words in the reading you just heard from 1 Corinthians; let's unpack them.

What is a temple?

Who or what is the Spirit of God?

And what are the implications for you of these words of St. Paul that apply directly to each one of you: "for the temple of God, which you are, is holy"?

First—what is a temple? It is sacred space. It is a building made sacred by God's presence.

Who or what is the Holy Spirit? This is part of a larger question—what is God like? As you know, our God is a Triune God—Father, Son, Holy Spirit. You know what a father is.

You can understand the meaning of a son. What about the Holy Spirit? What is God the Spirit like?

Well, Scripture describes the coming of the Spirit upon the apostles after the death of Jesus in imagery that is familiar to you—the Holy Spirit is like a flame, like the wind. Consider these words from the Acts of the Apostles, a book that is sometimes referred to as the second volume of Luke's work—the first is the Lucan Gospel and the second is the Book of Acts, which appears in the New Testament immediately after the four Gospels. In any case, listen to Acts, chapter 2: "When the time for Pentecost was fulfilled they [the disciples] were all in one place together. And suddenly there came from the sky a noise like a strong driving wind, and it filled the entire house in which they were. Then there appeared to them tongues as of fire, which parted and came to rest on each one of them. And they were all filled with the Holy Spirit and began to speak in different tongues, as the Spirit enabled them to proclaim" (vv. 1–4).

So what is God the Holy Spirit like? Well, first you might say like a breath, like a wind likely to make its presence known unexpectedly. The Holy Spirit is invisible—no matter, just spirit—immaterial but present to us.

The Holy Spirit is like a flame. The Spirit can fire us up. The Holy Spirit is sometimes referred to by theologians as the spirit of love between Father and Son. What might that mean? In a book called *This Is Our Faith: A Catholic Catechism for Adults* (Ave Maria Press), Michael Pennock, in speaking of the Holy Spirit, writes: "The relationship of the Father and Son is a perfect relationship. The Father and the Son love each other with an eternal, perfect, divine love. The love proceeds from the Father and the Son and is the third Person of the Trinity, the Holy Spirit. The Holy Spirit proceeds from both the Father and the Son as the perfect expression of their divine love for each other. Thus, the Holy Spirit is the spirit of love between the Father and the Son; the Spirit binds them into a community of unity."

This is a mystery of our faith. Theology tries to shed light on mystery, but...

Let's go back to where we began—

"Do you not know that you are the temple of God, and that the Spirit of God dwells in you? If anyone destroys God's temple, God will destroy that person; for the temple of God, which you are, is holy" (1 Cor 3:16–17).

And what are the implications for you of these words of St. Paul that apply directly to each one of you: "for the temple of God, which you are, is holy"?

Here are the implications: First, you are holy.... You are made holy by the presence within you of the Spirit of God—the Spirit of love between Father and Son. This is the reality of grace in your life. Grace means gift. You are gifted with God within you. You are a temple that houses this great gift.

Consider the implications of this in terms of required respect for yourself and respect for others.

Now, of course, you are a flesh-and-blood temple, not a brick-and-stone temple. You are nonetheless, a temple, a house of God.

How do you care for that temple? What goes on in that temple? Only you can answer those questions, but answer you must as you hear God's word to you today from 1 Corinthians.

Why are we—you and I, all of us—hesitant to seek holiness? Why are we afraid to admit that we are holy, that our bodies are sacred space? That we are destined—body and soul—to live forever?

These are profound truths, not inaccessible, just profound. Their profundity is a measure of their importance and the extent to which they deserve careful, prayerful, quiet consideration on the part of each one of us today.

I'll stop now so that you can begin to ponder, and so that the Holy Spirit who dwells within you can get to work enlightening your mind and lifting your spirit.

39

Eighth Sunday of the Year

Isaiah 49:14–15; Psalm 62; 1 Corinthians 4:1–5; Matthew 6:24–34

"YOU CANNOT SERVE GOD AND MAMMON"

This is the famous "two masters" Gospel, the age-old warning that you cannot serve both God and mammon; that word "mammon" is sometimes translated "money," hence you cannot serve both God and money. True, you cannot serve two masters at the same time. If you try, this Gospel message is telling you, you "will either hate one and love the other," or "be attentive to one and despise the other."

In order to process all this positively and productively, you have to take a realistic reading on your place in the world. You are here by God's design, by God's will. God created you and clearly God is your master. You acknowledge that, of course; you give daily praise and thanks to God. You acknowledge God as your creator. You are accordingly "attentive" to God; you also "love" God.

But does that mean you have to "hate" or "despise" the world and the things of the world, including money? After all, God created the world as well, and in doing so God saw that "it is good." Indeed the world is good. And as St. John's Gospel (3:16) reminds you, "For God so loved the world that he gave his only Son, so that everyone who believes in him might not perish but might have eternal life." Notice how all of us are included in that word St. John employs, he says, "everyone," and in doing so suggests that we are all part of the world that God loved so much.

Surely, then, you must not hate the world. But the world has ways of doing things—"man-made ways," we often say; and not all man-made ways are good. Moreover, human beings have, since the beginning, devised instruments to help themselves get things done—tools, for one example; the wheel for another. Money would be still another. And not all tools are always used wisely or well.

So it is worth taking a few minutes today to look at our way of using tools like money. It is worth reflecting upon the "ways of the world" and worldly values—this world's values—that might in fact be in opposition to otherworldly, Godly values. We have ways of doing things with money that are not all good. Money is intended to be a store of value and a medium of exchange, but money can be used to bribe, money can be used overpower others, money can be used to paper over personal deficits of character and intelligence, or to put it another way, to try to impress others and thus purchase their admiration and esteem. Money can feed our greedy appetites; just pile it up, watch it grow. Money can be hoarded. Net worth can be mistaken for human worth. Money can lock us in, cut us off, shut us down; money can make misers of us all. This worldly reality is hardly what God would call good!

You need money to live, but you cannot allow yourself to identify the accumulation of money with the meaning of life. You may even be well-off, as we say, but you must not permit yourself to become so well-off that you remove yourself from interest in or contact with the poor. In trying to balance your relationship to God and money, you have to keep in mind that you are fully capable of letting yourself become possessed by your possessions. There is a trap out there waiting to spring, waiting to ensnare you. And guess who is out there setting those traps for the unsuspecting sojourners moving through this world? The trap-setter is the enemy of your human nature, Satan.

Your human nature is attracted to money and the things that money can buy. Nothing wrong with that. Your human nature enjoys the esteem in which those who possess money are held. That's understandable, but the acquisitive side of your human nature must be held in check. You cannot serve both God and money, which is not to say that you cannot use money wisely and well in your service of God. You can. You must.

Balance is not always easy to achieve. We live in an unbalanced society; we lead, many of us, unbalanced lives. The Church is inviting you today to think about the balance between matter and spirit, between

God and money in your life. Not just your life, but the lives of those around you also. You who are parents should certainly be thinking about how to encourage that balance in the minds and hearts of your children. Is that balance reflected in their lives, in their choices? Or, are they infected by the virus of materialism? Quite possibly they are and if they are, that should be a matter of major concern.

A wealthy grandfather said to me recently, "We have deprived our children and grandchildren of deprivation." His childhood included deprivations imposed by the Great Depression. He acknowledged his failure in later years to recognize the value of deprivation—not destitution, by any means, just the normal limits of deprivation—in the lives of his growing children and grandchildren whom we would call children of affluence. He saw now their need for the kind of self-imposed deprivation that makes better persons of us all. Unwittingly, he permitted his children and grandchildren to grow up with a sense of entitlement that inserted dollar signs into their way of spelling success, and viewed car keys as the only keys to happiness.

It is extremely hard to undo this kind of early life experience, to rework this malformation of character. But this work must be done and can be done through academic and athletic discipline, through voluntary community service, through exposure to the realities of life that the poor and powerless experience on a daily basis.

So Jesus is asking you to be thoughtful and reflective today as you ponder the implications of this Gospel warning. He is also asking you to lift your eyes so that you can consider the "birds of the air" and lift your hearts so that you can "learn a lesson from the way the wild flowers grow. They do not work; they do not spin….If God can clothe in such splendor the grass of the field…will he not provide much more for you?"

Indeed he will—for you, your children, and grandchildren. But let all generations of believers recommit themselves to God as their master, and recognize money as a necessary tool to be used wisely, which means moderately, on a faith-filled journey through a balanced life.

40

Ninth Sunday of the Year

Deuteronomy 11:18, 26–28; Psalm 31; Romans 3:21–25, 28;
Matthew 7:21–27

DOING GOD'S WILL; BUILDING ON ROCK

This typical Sunday Gospel—a selection from the Gospel of
Matthew—begins as so many Gospel readings do with the words,
"Jesus said to his disciples." Those words invite you to get into that
audience, so to speak, to think of yourselves as disciples, as students
of Jesus, followers of Jesus; and his words invite you to put yourselves
in an attentive mode, a listening posture, so that you can pay attention
to what your master wants to say to you, to listen to what your teacher
wants to teach, to benefit from what your friend Jesus has to share with
you. You can always count on wisdom being associated with what Jesus
has to say. You can always count on what he has to say being in some
way relevant to your daily life.

So, listen up; be attentive; don't let the Gospel proclamation fly over
your head or simply go unheeded.

In today's Gospel reading Jesus says to his disciples, "Not everyone
who says to me, 'Lord, Lord,' will enter the kingdom of heaven, but only
the one who does the will of my Father in heaven." Well, that should
have gotten their attention, as indeed today it should get yours. It is a
fairly stern message. The stakes are high. We're talking about eternal life,
the kingdom of God. You can't just say, "Lord, Lord, I'd like to get there;
I'd like to have a place in the kingdom; I hope you'll count me in." No;
wishing won't make it so. Just petitioning the Lord won't do it. More is
required. Only those who do the will of the Father are going to make it.

You have to think seriously about aligning your will with the will of
your Father in heaven—all the time. What does God will for you? How

141

serious are you about seeking out the will of God? Do you even know how to begin to seek out the will of God? That's a question worthy of consideration today. That's a really important question: How do you seek and find the will of God for you?

You can begin to read God's will in a very general way by just considering the gifts you have, your created self, the talents and powers that are yours in virtue of your creaturehood. If you are male, God could hardly have willed that you become a mother. If you are five-feet, five-inches tall, God could hardly have willed that you be a basketball player in the NBA. If you have a high IQ, God might have willed that you be a research scientist, but if you love poetry and hate physics, that may be God's way of telling you that you should follow the path of the humanities and avoid the heavy traffic on the road of math, engineering, and science. If you can't stand the sight of blood, God is probably not expecting you to be a nurse. And so it goes as you take an inventory of what you have, what you like, what engages your interest.

You have to let yourself take an honest look at your deep-down desires—what is it that your best self hopes for, longs for? What is it that you enjoy and really like? If you say I really like drinking and gambling and high-speed joy rides, you cannot assume that you have discovered God's will for you. You first have to locate your best self, your true self, your generous self, made in the image and likeness of God, and then ask what that best self really seeks. It may well be that God is there waiting to be found in that search, in that seeking.

That's what I mean by the challenge we all face of aligning our individual wills with the will of God. Today's Gospel puts it this way: "Not everyone who says to me, 'Lord, Lord,' will enter the kingdom of heaven but only the one who does the will of my Father in heaven." So give some serious thought and quiet prayer to the important issue of seeking and finding God's will for you at every stage of your life. Don't let yourself sleepwalk through life; be attentive to the will of God for you every step of the way.

Now, in this same Gospel story, Jesus offers you some reassuring words: "Everyone who listens to these words of mine and acts on them [in other words, anyone who is doing what you are doing right now!], will be like a wise man who built his house on rock. The rain fell, the floods came, and the winds blew and buffeted his house. But it did not collapse; it had been set solidly on rock."

You can picture scenes of high winds and drenching rains. You may have witnessed them first hand on the ground at some point in your life; you've surely seen them in television news coverage of hurricanes and tsunamis. You know what tornadoes can do. So, take care to hear the word of the Lord and keep it. If you do, you've built your house on solid rock. You'll withstand the storm.

"Everyone who listens to these words of mine but does *not* act on them will be like a fool who built his house on sand. The rain fell, the floods came, and the winds blew and buffeted the house. And it collapsed and was completely ruined." You can easily picture that scene; you know what the Lord is trying to tell you. He is saying that you must be attentive to his word and that you must be responsive to his will for you. Otherwise, you are walking in quicksand; you are risking the collapse of everything!

It is reassuring then to know that you can hear God's word by "listening" to sacred Scripture—not just when you are gathered for liturgy, but anytime in the quiet of your heart and home. Listen, and God will surely speak to you.

Similarly, you have the assurance of knowing that if you sincerely seek the will of God, if you do your best to align your will with the will of God, you will make the right choices and follow the path of God's will for you. How can you know that you are on the right path, that you have discovered God's will for you? There is a certain confirmatory contentment—not complacency by any means—but a sense of peace that you can feel—literally feel—and it will reinforce you, uphold you, strengthen you, and convince you that you and God are in alignment— heart to heart, will to will. Seek spiritual direction if you need help in sorting these things out. Make a weekend retreat if you can.

Let yourself be convinced not only that God made you and that God loves you, but that God wills your happiness here and your salvation hereafter. Do your best to connect your will with the will of God as you make your way, and enjoy the security of that house built on rock as God's gift to you in your transit through life.

41

Tenth Sunday of the Year

Hosea 6:3–6; Psalm 50; Romans 4:18–25; Matthew 9:9–13

"I DESIRE MERCY, NOT SACRIFICE"

"Those who are well do not need a physician," says Jesus in this morning's selection from Matthew's Gospel, "but the sick do," he notes. "Go and learn the meaning of the words, 'I desire mercy, not sacrifice,'" says Jesus to the Pharisees who criticized him for dining with social outcasts, with "tax collectors and sinners" (the tax collectors were hated and shunned because they were collaborators of the Roman imperial authorities; they also exploited the people by collecting more than they should).

"I desire mercy, not sacrifice." Those words were originally spoken by the prophet Hosea; or, to put it more accurately, spoken by God through the prophet Hosea. In Hosea chapter 6, verse 6, you will hear the Lord say, through the voice of the prophet, "For it is love that I desire, not sacrifice, and knowledge of God, rather than holocausts." This is the thought, the conviction, that Jesus wants to communicate to his critics as he, Jesus, sits at table surrounded by social outcasts.

Would you be uncomfortable at that table, in that company? Jesus apparently was not. In placing himself in the company of sinners, social outcasts, Jesus made a break with the Pharisees, with religious leaders of the past. This story shows something of the novelty, the originality of his ministry, not to mention the dimensions of his mercy. He reaches out to the marginalized; he welcomes the outcasts.

I guess we all have occasion from time to time to take comfort in that fact, those of us who have known the need for a spiritual physician. We take comfort from the fact that God desires mercy, not sacrifice, even though we offer sacrifice to atone for our sins as a way of asking for mercy. "I desire mercy, not sacrifice," says Jesus. "Those who are well do not need a physician, but the sick do," he says.

What might these words mean to us today? What might these words have meant to the Catholic bishops of the United States when they formulated and evaluated the policy document that affects the fate and future of sinners and social outcasts in the ranks of Catholic clergy and in the ranks of the bishops themselves, those who made the headlines in recent years for crimes of committing or covering up acts of sexual molestation of minors?

"Off with all their heads," do I hear you say? Zero tolerance for past as well as future offenders? One strike and out you go, regardless of time served, reparations made, debts paid, remorse expressed, psychological fitness certified? I speak in the interrogative, not declarative mode, because I want you to turn those questions over in your hearts today. Set aside your biases. Be judicious and deliberative, and just because you are deliberative, let no one accuse you of favoring the accused and being insensitive to the abused. Dampen down your anger and outrage. Pray for the bishops, for the victims, for the perpetrators. Realize that it will take wisdom and an enormous amount of courage for the bishops to decide wisely and fairly in this area. So pray that the decisions the bishops have taken, and will have to take in the future, are taken in accord with the will of God and the work of the Holy Spirit.

There is a little-noticed prayer that the priest says in each Mass immediately before receiving the Eucharist. "Lord Jesus Christ, son of the living God," he prays, "by the will of the Father and the work of the Holy Spirit, your death brought life to the world. By your holy body and blood free me from all my sins, and from every evil. Keep me faithful to your teaching, and never let me be parted from you." That translation has been slightly revised in the new Roman Missal. It's a beautiful prayer. There is resurrection theology in it. We move through death to life; Christ's death brought life to the world.

The priest prays, "Never let me be parted from you." This is not to suggest that some priests should not be separated from their priesthood. It is to suggest, however, that out of this "death" in our time, out of this scandal, out of this sexual abuse crisis, new "life" will come, and it will come to our Church and our world "by the will of the Father and the work of the Holy Spirit."

We are not abandoned. We are not helpless and alone. As outrageous and wrong the actions that caused this crisis are, as morally and emotionally sick the perpetrators have been, as inept and perhaps even corrupt official decision making may have been, there is still hope. "[W]here sin increased, grace overflowed all the more" wrote Paul to the Romans (5:20). Those words speak to us today.

May grace abound. May divine wisdom strike the right balance between mercy and sacrifice. And may Christ be present always to teach our bishops, successors to his apostles, "the meaning of the words, 'I desire mercy, not sacrifice.'" Whatever those words do in fact mean, they won't mean much if they fail to spell out justice for all.

42

Eleventh Sunday of the Year

Exodus 19:2–6; Psalm 100; Romans 5:6–11; Matthew 9:36—10:8

"ASK THE MASTER OF THE HARVEST TO SEND OUT LABORERS FOR HIS HARVEST"

Today's Gospel reading provides us with an opportunity to think about vocations to priesthood and religious life. Let me acknowledge right at the outset that the vocation question has much broader application than just to priesthood and religious life. I'm fully aware of that. Every one of you has a vocation; God is, and has all your life long, been calling you. A call is a vocation. You have one. You have to respond. God has called and will continue to call most of you to marriage, as well as to specific ways to earn a living and, through your work, to serve your brothers and sisters in the human community. Some of you are called to teach, to nurse, to heal, to promote and protect just relationships through the law; some are called to design and build, to buy and sell, to govern, to entertain, to research and discover, to the farm or the factory—there is a very long list of ways in which God calls you to live your life while here on earth.

Not everyone has a vocation to priesthood or religious life. But some do. And today I want to speak to and about them. The context of today's Gospel story provides a congenial setting for us to consider the call to priesthood and religious life.

First, you notice that Jesus "was moved with pity" at the sight of the crowds. They appeared to him to be like "sheep without a shepherd." And then you see him turn to his disciples and say to them: "The harvest is abundant but the laborers are few; so ask the master of the harvest to send out laborers for his harvest."

There were no nuns, as we know them, when Jesus lived; there were no priests in service to the Church then either. In fact there was not yet a Church. But we can still with confidence say that Jesus had in mind the need for priests and religious in his Church when he spoke of the harvest being ready but not having enough laborers to gather it in. He had then, as he walked this earth, an unimaginably large agenda in mind. He was out to bring the good news of salvation to the entire human race, to bring all men and women back to the Father and home to heaven. And he had a plan that would unfold over time for establishing a Church, a caring community of believers, and calling members of that Church to special service—to priesthood and religious life in the Church—all in pursuit of that overarching goal, the salvation of the human race. But he wasn't out just to save souls; he wanted to save bodies too. That's why the Church has had its schools, hospitals, social services, and other direct-assistance ministries.

Over the centuries, men and women of faith, generosity, and zeal saw the great need for laborers to bring in that harvest Jesus spoke about and they offered their services to the Church by becoming priests and religious who, like their Master, realized that they were on this earth "not to be served, but to serve, and to give their lives as a ransom for many" (Matt 20:28). Special persons whom we call saints emerged in the history of the Church. Some of them, like Francis of Assisi, Benedict, Dominic, and Ignatius of Loyola, established religious communities whose members would imitate Christ by pronouncing the vows of poverty, chastity, and obedience, and offer themselves to provide service along lines envisioned by their respective founders. Other religious communities adopted names that honored characteristics of Mary the Mother of God, like the Sisters of St. Mary; or Jesus himself, like the Redemptorists or the Congregation of the Holy Cross; or great saints like Joseph, Paul, and Augustine—you've heard of the Josephites, the Paulists, and the Augustinians.

There was such a multiplication of religious orders, communities, and congregations of men and women in the history of the Church that Catholics often joked that only God knew how many there actually were. And there has been remarkable multiplication of geographic jurisdictions called "dioceses" all around the world that recruit and train so-called "diocesan" priests or secular clergy who do not pronounce religious vows or follow a monastic style of life. There still are countless religious communities that are welcoming new recruits to assist in the task of bringing in the harvest. And there are impressive numbers of diocesan priests throughout the world to minister to the people of God. But their numbers are declining. There are fewer priests and religious today than there were a generation or two ago. There is concern now in the Church about our ability to maintain ministry to the people of God. So the question about the availability of laborers to bring in the harvest is very much on the Catholic mind—at least on many Catholic minds, although it should be a concern for all.

An August 21, 2011, headline in the *New York Times* caught my eye: "Nuns, a 'Dying Breed,' Fade from Leadership Roles at Catholic Hospitals." Here is the opening paragraph of that story: "When Sister Mary Jean Ryan entered the convent as a young nurse in 1960, virtually every department of every Catholic hospital was run by a nun, from pediatrics to dietary to billing. After her retirement on July 31 [2011] as the chief executive of one of the country's largest networks of Catholic hospitals, only 11 nuns remained among her company's more than 22,000 employees, and none were administrators."

Ponder the implications of those numbers as you move on to consider the second paragraph of the news story, which ran under a St. Louis dateline: "For SSM [Sisters of St. Mary] Health Care, a $4.2 billion enterprise that evolved from the work of five German nuns who arrived here in 1872, Sister Mary Jean's departure after 25 years as the company's first chief executive marks a poignant passing. The gradual transition from religious to lay leadership, which has been changing the face of Catholic health care for decades, is now nearly complete."

From five immigrant nuns 140 years ago to a 22,000 employee healthcare system in 2011 is quite a transition. What might five nuns decide to do today, if they wanted to serve God's people? Where might five committed, venturesome, Catholic women band together to undertake such work today? Not in Sister Mary Jean's order. It, according to the Times story, "has dwindled to about 100 from a peak of more than 500. Most moved out of their convent last year and into a retirement and nursing home. There has not been an initiate [novice] for 25 years, and several years ago the sisters reluctantly stopped looking."

The decision was "painful," says Sister Mary Jean, "but I think it was also courageous to say we're just not going to recruit any more. Let's just live out the rest of our lives to the fullest that we possibly can and thank God for what we've been able to do. And when the time comes, as they say, let the last person turn the lights out."

Is God still calling young men and women to religious life? Yes indeed. I don't know that every existing religious order can count on a continuing flow of recruits. Some of the orders have to adapt to new circumstances. Some will cease to exist. And some new orders will have to emerge to meet new needs. The spectacle of happy men and women doing useful work will continue to attract the generous young to religious life. The sight of great fields of human need awaiting harvest will be there for potential harvesters to see. The question is: will they respond to the call?

Attention must also be paid to the declining ranks of diocesan priests. The first decade of the twenty-first century saw the outbreak of the greatest crisis the Catholic Church in the United States has ever known. That crisis, namely the clergy sex abuse scandal, has touched the Church in other countries as well. It is a genuine crisis and one hardly suited to creating an attractive environment for the recruiting of candidates for priesthood. But God is still calling men to priesthood. The need for more good men—generous, healthy, talented men who have a high-hearted love for Christ and his people—is urgent in the Church today. Where sin abounds, as St. Paul once said, grace abounds all the more. And it is certain that the grace of a vocation to priesthood is there awaiting a response from the young and generous as we speak.

So think about it, you who are young; and you who are not so young should be praying for more vocations to priesthood and religious life. Pray to the Lord of the harvest that he will send more laborers into the ranks of priesthood and religious life, and pray that those called will be open to working not just for, but with, laypersons who have their own vocations and, in God's providence, are also called to working in and with the Church in its ministry for the salvation of the world.

43

Twelfth Sunday of the Year

Jeremiah 20: 10–13; Psalm 69; Romans 5:12–15; Matthew 10:26–33

FEAR NO ONE

The opening words of today's Gospel passage have Jesus saying to the Twelve, and derivatively down through the centuries to you: "Fear no one." How do you react to that directive? "Fear no one," he says, and then goes on to assert: "Nothing is concealed that will not be revealed, nor secret that will not be known."

If you're like me, you may be saying that you don't find those words all that reassuring; they in fact give you some cause for fear. But he repeats his instruction: "Fear no one." "Do not be afraid," this Gospel tells you, "of those who kill the body but cannot kill the soul; rather be afraid of the one who can destroy both soul and body in Gehenna."

Jesus is putting some serious considerations before you today. He also offers you hope and encouragement with the reminder that "you are worth more than many sparrows," the sparrow does not "fall to the ground without your Father's knowledge," and, presumably, without your Father's caring providence, the providence that he has in infinitely greater measure for you.

Let's face up to fear for a few moments today. At least let's think, in the light of today's Gospel, about our experience of fear in everyday life.

Fear is part of the coin you need to pay your dues for membership in the human race. No one can go through life without the experience of fear.

Fear makes the positive contribution of defending (or at least warning) you against danger. In the ordinary, everyday, common sense meaning of the word, fear can weigh you down, knock you out, hold

151

you back, destroy your peace of mind, force you to withdraw, and rob your heart of happiness. The Christian tradition reminds those who are faithful but also fearful, that love can drive out fear. In the First Letter of John (4:18–19) you will read: "There is no fear in love, but perfect love drives out fear because fear has to do with punishment, and so one who fears is not yet perfect in love. We love because he first loved us." Keep that in mind as you think about fear in your life.

A not-so-ordinary and far less obvious understanding of the word would equate fear with reverence. "Fear of the Lord," a familiar expression in several religious traditions, should be understood in this way. Your reverence before the Lord is an expression of fear of the Lord. This is not servile fear, and most assuredly not neurotic fear. It is reverence in the face of an awe-inspiring reality, namely, the presence of an all-knowing, all-powerful, all-loving God in your life.

What a distortion of this special meaning of fear when someone threatens to "put the fear of God in you!" God is never to be feared in a display of fright-filled cowering on your part. You show your fear of God in reverence. Fear your own capacity to reject your God, but have no fear that God will ever reject you.

"Fearless" is a quality often attributed to persons who do heroic things. Sometimes those who seem to be fearless are insufficiently aware (perhaps too dumb to comprehend) the real danger in a given situation. But when all the hazards are noted and fully understood, the one who is "fearless," is one who has overcome fear, not one who is without fear.

Most of us have to learn how to manage our fears as we move forward, rather than permitting fear to hold us back. A rabbit's foot is no guarantee of safe passage. Putting your own foot forward, despite the fears that seem to be closing in on you, is the only way to go.

Of what are you afraid? What fears weigh you down? Make mental notes or jot them down on paper. You'll probably find yourself sorting them out in general categories like health, money, and work, or in more personal folders that catalogue your phobias. That will be like looking at yourself in a house of mirrors. Be fair enough to yourself to acknowledge that the images those mirrors throw back are distorted (exaggerated fears?). You can work out the distortions with professional help, if you need it, or by just laughing at yourself (as everyone does in a house of mirrors) and moving on.

It's been said that anyone who harbors habitual fear is "landlord to a ghost." The point is worth considering. Some of your fears point to the past, but the past is dead (it's a ghost). Some point to the future, but the future may never arrive, at least not in the form that you now anticipate (that ghost may never show up). Why permit an invisible enemy like fear to pull you out of the present moment, the only moment that is fully in your possession?

Most of that which you fear does not exist, at least does not exist in the present moment, the only place where you live. You have to remember that a life lived in fear is a life half-lived, so handing yourself over to present fears means giving up a valuable portion of your life. Handing yourself over to fears of the past puts you in the custody of a ghost. And turning yourself over to fears about the future "gives up the ghost," as they say, leaving you helpless and, go ahead and say it— afraid. It makes no sense.

You can make a lot of sense by taking charge of your life, which is another way of saying, taking charge of your fears. If you have trouble doing that, get professional help. If you can do it with difficulty, get to work right now because it will not be easier at any time in the future.

Take a minute now, as we prepare to offer out gifts at the altar, to pray your fears down to manageable size. And permit me to lead you in that prayer with these words:

Fear of failure.
Fear of the dark.
Fear of illness.
Fear of rejection.
Fear of discovery.
Fear of speaking up, or out, or saying it in public.
Fear of losing my job.
Fear of harm to those I love.
Fear of hating those who do me harm.
Fear of heights, of depths, of water, and of fire.
Fear of falling.

Fear of abandonment, engulfment, annihilation,
Fear of those who want (I think) to do me harm.

Why should I be afraid of all these, Lord, and of so much more?
It can only be because I think I'm altogether on my own,
placing myself away from you, out of touch, and out of reach.
The power is yours, Lord; certain tasks are mine.
I'll do what I can; I'll muddle through somehow,
because I believe that you are here with me and I have nothing
    to fear.
Nothing.
Amen.

"Jesus said to the Twelve: Fear no one. Nothing is concealed that will not be revealed, nor secret that will not be known...[D]o not be afraid of those who kill the body but cannot kill the soul; rather, be afraid of the one who can destroy both soul and body in Gehenna.... So do not be afraid; you are worth more than many sparrows."

44

Thirteenth Sunday of the Year

2 Kings 4:8–11, 14–16; Psalm 89; Romans 6:3–4, 8–11;
Matthew 10:37–42

ON LOSING YOUR LIFE IN ORDER TO FIND IT

Turn over in your minds for a few minutes right now the words Matthew puts on the lips of Jesus in the Gospel selection you just heard: "whoever loses his [or her] life for my sake will find it." This is one of the riddles of Christianity. It is in giving that we receive, Jesus tells us. If you want to find your life, try losing it.

Let's reflect together on the riddle of losing your life in order to find it.

When we use the expression in ordinary speech, "losing" one's life, means dying. "He lost his life in the Twin Towers." "She lost her life on Flight 83." "They were among those who lost their lives in the terrorist attack on the Pentagon on September 11, 2001." "How many lives were lost in the Vietnam War?" And so it goes in ordinary speech. But in the religious discourse prompted by this Gospel proclamation, "losing life" means something quite different. You don't die when you take Jesus up on this promise. You find your life. You begin living life more fully as the function of a decision you made that has all the outward appearances of a choice against self.

Every one of you, I suspect, is searching for the meaning of your life at every age and stage of that life. You are always trying to unravel the mystery of life. That may be why you're here, at the altar, in God's presence. You wonder about the deeper meaning of life.

What is life? You've all heard that question sung in the words of "What's It All About, Alfie?" Well, I think we are meant to be kind, and I'm sure you will agree. We are meant to be kind and, at times, being kind means saying no to self. We are not meant to take more than we give. And the source of this meaning is the source of life, our Triune God, who gave his only Son as an explanation of life, as a pattern to be followed by those in search of the good life, the happy life, the meaningful life. Follow Christ and you will soon notice that the happy life is the life lived generously in the service of others.

Jesus taught this lesson of the meaning of life in his own way of living life on earth as well as in the words he left for our instruction. He used images to teach, as you well know, and one of those images that conveys this lesson is the simple everyday agricultural example of the grain of wheat: "Unless the wheat grain falls to the ground and dies, it remains just a single grain of wheat, but if it dies, it produces much fruit" (John 12:24). Just another way of saying, "whoever loses his [or her] life for my sake will find it," in the workplace, in marriage and the family, in fatherhood, motherhood, priesthood, in any one of a wide variety of ministries.

We walk by faith not by sight—so if you don't see this at first glance that losing your life is the way to find it, if you don't "get it," "buy into it," if it doesn't add up for you, make sense to you, don't strain to "see"; just try to believe. Ease up, calm down, cool your engine, take a break, and let your believing be your seeing.

The life you are now living, the busy but not necessarily happy life you know, may be what the poet Linda Pastan had in mind in her poetic salute to what happens on a stationary bicycle: "…this ride feels/ much like life itself going nowhere/ strenuously." Perhaps you feel that way, that you are "going nowhere strenuously." That is not Christ's plan for you. That is not the way that he, who is the way, the truth, and the life, laid out for you.

He doesn't prescribe passivity for you, but he does recommend patience—patience with the laws of growth, for instance, the kind of patience that is part of the wheat grain's growth toward fruitfulness.

Christ would also have you look at yourself in relationship to him. In the light of himself who is the Light of the World, you will gain a better sense of yourself and your place in his plans for the world. In trying to grasp what I am suggesting here, take a look at the life of St. Thomas More.

In the preface to the American edition of his play *A Man for All Seasons* Robert Bolt explains that Thomas More, "as I wrote about him, became for me a man with an adamantine sense of his own self. He knew where he began and where he left off, what area of himself he could yield to the encroachments of his enemies, and what to the encroachments of those he loved…but [he would not] retreat from the final area where he located his self. And there this supple, humorous, unassuming and sophisticated person set like metal, was overtaken by an absolutely primitive rigor, and could no more be budged than a cliff."

Bolt goes on to note that Thomas More "found something in himself without which life was valueless and when that was denied him was able to grasp his death." "Why," asks Bolt "do I take as my hero a man who brings about his own death because he can't put his hand on an old black book and tell an ordinary lie? For this reason: A man takes an oath only when he wants to commit himself quite exceptionally to the statement, when he wants to make an identity between the truth of it and his own virtue; he offers himself as a guarantee. And it worked. There is a special kind of shrug for a perjurer; we feel that the man has no self to commit, no guarantee to offer." For Robert Bolt, Thomas More was a hero of selfhood.

I'm inviting you to think of yourself now and your selfhood as you might think of your manhood or your womanhood. Think of what selfhood means to you. Selfhood is altogether different from self-centeredness, or selfishness. It is character, the bedrock of personal commitment and the precondition of personal and societal security. Your own character has to be the basis of your response to the instability and unpredictability of our times. And part of your character, if indeed you are a Christian, will be the values communicated to you in the Gospel of Jesus Christ.

In the "losing-life, finding-life" framework of today's Gospel, listen to words I want to read now that translate this Christian value system into terms familiar to us all. This is a reflection, a prayer found, I'm told, on the dead body of a soldier who lost his life in the Civil War. I can't vouch for that. I simply offer these words as a perspective-setter, a balancing factor for anyone who is searching for life's deeper meaning:

> I asked God for strength, that I might achieve.
> I was made weak, that I might learn to obey.
> I asked for health, that I might do greater things.
> I was given infirmity, that I might do better things.
> I asked for riches, that I might be happy.
> I was given poverty, that I might be wise.
> I asked for power, that I might have the praise of men.
> I was given weakness, that I might feel the need of God.
> I asked for all things, that I might enjoy life.
> I was given life, that I might enjoy all things.
> I got nothing that I asked for but everything I had hoped for.
> Almost despite myself, my unspoken prayers were answered.
> I am, among all men, most richly blessed.

The fourth psalm says, "Know that the Lord works wonders for the faithful." Let the Lord work the wonder within you of losing your selfishness in order to gain your selfhood, and, like the wheat grain, letting your life fall, as if to die, into the ground of service, only to produce fruit in quantities that you cannot now even begin to imagine.

45

Fourteenth Sunday of the Year

Zechariah 9:9–10; Psalm 145; Romans 8:9, 11–13; Matthew 11:25–30

"COME TO ME, ALL YOU WHO LABOR AND ARE BURDENED"

Today, or any day of the year, it is deeply comforting to hear the Lord Jesus speak directly to you and say, "Come to me all you who labor and are burdened, and I will give you rest." That is the heart of today's Gospel message.

You may not feel particularly weary at the moment, and perhaps you do not find life particularly burdensome today, but you've been there in the past and are likely to experience those feelings in the future; so savor the words of Jesus today and let them seep into the inner recesses of your soul: "Come to me all you who labor and are burdened." When the weight of worry settles down upon you, you know where to go!

Weariness comes and goes at all stages of your life; it seems to linger, bordering on the permanent, as you grow older. Discouragement can accompany weariness; at times that discouragement can gravitate toward despair. Similarly, life can become burdensome with shifting intensity from time to time. Some carry the burden of illness. Others the burden of decision making. Deadlines burden some of you. Unemployment can surely be a burden. So can the death of a dear one or reversal of fortunes in business for you or someone close to you. Concerns about the economic security of your family can certainly become burdensome, as can worries about the ability of your children to choose wisely and well as they encounter temptation and find themselves at important decision points in their young lives. And as those of you who are closer to the end than to the beginning know so well, the burden of loneliness in old age can weigh heavily upon you.

You know where to go whenever those burdens begin to feel unmanageable. Go in prayer to Jesus. Meet him also in the sacraments. Never yield to the temptation that tries to convince you that you are alone, on your own, left to your own resources. No, you've got reliable support, a true and powerful friend in the one who says to you today, "Come to me all you who labor and are burdened, and I will give you rest." I will shore you up, he says. I will provide light and guidance. I will show you the way.

Every Liturgy of the Word offers us a Responsorial Psalm to consider, yet all too often we hardly hear let alone assimilate the words, forgetting that these are inspired words from Scripture; they come from the Holy Spirit. Today, for instance, Psalm 145 speaks wise words to you: "The Lord is gracious and merciful, / slow to anger and of great kindness. / The Lord is good to all / and compassionate toward all his works." You are one of his works; he can be nothing but good and compassionate toward you. So turn to him in your need. "The Lord is faithful in all his words," the psalmist goes on to say, "and holy in all his works. / The Lord lifts up all who are falling / and raises up all who are bowed down." You can hardly afford to ignore these divinely inspired and reassuring words; you are surely the loser if you let them pass unheeded.

Jesus knew a lot about the human condition even though he was on this earth for only thirty-three years. He knew that most of us would have longer life spans and his preaching—intended for all of us down through the ages—acknowledged that we were in it for the long haul and he was exquisitely sensitive to the fact that we had to work our way—not without worry and not burden free—through the human predicament. So he could say to us, as he does in today's short Gospel message, "Take my yoke upon you and learn from me, for I am meek and humble of heart and your soul will find rest for yourselves. For my yoke is easy and my burden light."

The key is to do it his way—bravely and courageously. He walked the way of the cross, and so can you. He presented himself as gentle and humble and he, in effect, said that gentleness and humility are the way we should walk. He was and is a leader of unparalleled success, but he led from gentleness and humility, not power, prestige, wealth, and arrogance. And he is saying to us who hear this Gospel today that wherever you lead—at home in the family, at school, business, government, the military, in the private voluntary sector—wherever you lead, realize that you are there to serve and to do so gently and with humility.

Humility is strength, not weakness; it is all too often confused with timidity. But humility, as exemplified in the life and Jesus, is true courage. And so is gentleness—that admirable attentiveness to the needs of others that the gentle person consistently demonstrates—gentleness is strength. These are countercultural values in contemporary society. If you define a culture by its dominant value, you would have to say that in today's business culture, greed is a dominant value; competition, not cooperation, is the way to go. If you look at military culture you see power dominating. In the entertainment culture it is pleasure—often lust—that dominates. So the Catholic Christian is invited to be countercultural when invited by Jesus to be meek and humble of heart, as he was. How does the contemporary Catholic pull that off?

I would suggest a new and unfamiliar word for your consideration today. It offers a key to how the Christian in the world of work—in the real world of Monday-through-Friday, nine-to-five, paycheck-responsibility days that are more than familiar to you—a key to how you can hold onto your basic Christian values—humility and gentleness—and still be effective, indeed successful, in meeting what we like to think of as our "real world" responsibilities. And that word is "humbition." It is an amalgam of two words—"humility" and "ambition." You have to be humbitious in order to be successful; you should be humbitious if you want to be Christlike in the world of work. He was surely humble. He was also ambitious for the salvation of the world, for the coming of the promised kingdom, for the salvation of souls.

So, be humble; and be ambitious for the glory of God and the salvation of souls. This will work for you at every stage of life, even in retirement. Think "humbition" and you will be on the right track to a good and richly rewarding life, remembering, of course, that when weariness sets in and the burdens become heavy, Jesus, the model of humbition, is there waiting to hear from you and more than ready to help.

46

Fifteenth Sunday of the Year

Isaiah 55:10–11; Psalm 65; Romans 8:18–23; Matthew 13:1–23

SOME SEED FELL ON RICH SOIL

Jesus had a way of telling stories in everyday language, using images that his hearers could easily understand. He spoke in parables, which are extended similes. He taught by moving from the familiar to the unfamiliar, from everyday experience to new understandings. He dealt in comparisons, as in this present instance where he compares a sower to a teacher, seed to the lesson to be learned, and different types of ground to different kinds of students, to different degrees of readiness to grasp the lesson being taught.

The language and images he employed do not always match up easily with our modern twenty-first–century experience, however. We don't know much about Palestinian agricultural society. We are not likely to know, for example, that in the Middle East when Jesus walked the earth, the land was not always plowed, as we would expect it to be in preparation for the planting of seed. The sower just went out and tossed the seed over good land and bad, over well-worn paths and even over rocky ground, as well as over soil that was ready and receptive.

It is easy enough for us nonetheless to get the point of this Gospel story. The seed is the word of God. It is the good news, the Gospel of life and hope, the good news of salvation, the way of forgiveness and sacrifice that he traced out for our guidance.

The seed that Christ our Sower sowed when he walked among us is a value system, a set of guidelines and principles for living the good life, the happy life, the productive life that leads to life everlasting. The seed he sowed offers guidance to corporate executives, to fathers and mothers, to accountants, priests, professional athletes, to entertainers and educators, to government officials, to scientists and principled engineers, to little people and big, to people young and old in all circumstances, in all times, and in all corners of the world.

Christ sowed his seed everywhere, generously intending it for everyone from his own day down through the centuries to the end of time. For everyone.

Hence everyone in every age would do well to pay attention to preparation, to the plowing, to the receptivity in his or her own heart for the lessons the Lord in his goodness wants to sow there. Think of how you prepare yourself in other ways, in other areas of life. You exercise to get into better physical shape. You go on diets from time to time. (I have a friend who went on a month-long diet and later complained that all he lost was thirty days! You know the feeling.) You also know that it is important to condition yourself, to cultivate, to prepare.

Wherever the Gospel is proclaimed throughout the world, the sower is there, still at work, sowing his seed. Listen again to the Gospel story: "And as he sowed, some seed fell on the path, and birds came and ate it up. Some fell on rocky ground, where it had little soil. It sprang up at once because the soil was not deep, and when the sun rose it was scorched, and it withered for lack of roots. Some fell among thorns, and the thorns grew up and choked it. But some seed fell on rich soil, and produced fruit, a hundred or sixty or thirty fold."

Some of you are gardeners. Think of yourself as the soil in your own garden. You need preparation, cultivation. You need some attention and it is you who should be attending to your own preparation and cultivation in the garden of your heart and mind where Gospel principles grow. Do what you must to make yourself rich soil, fertile ground. "But the seed sown on rich soil is the one who hears the word and understands it, who indeed bears fruit and yields a hundred or sixty or thirty fold."

Passivity never produced good garden growth. Inattention never yielded a crop.

Harvests don't just happen. You've got work to do.

First you have to attend to the suggestions the Sower is making for you here in today's Gospel. If you are like the path that some seed fell upon, then the Lord is pointing out to you that you've been hearing the word of the kingdom without understanding it, and "the evil one comes and steals away what was sown in [your] heart." Beware of the evil one. Don't ever deceive yourself into thinking that you are not a target of the evil one. Don't be fooled into thinking that there is no "evil one" at work today in your world.

If you are offering rocky ground to the falling seed, then you're the one "who hears the word and receives it at once with joy. But [you have] no root and [the seed] lasts only for a time. When some tribulation or persecution comes because of the word, [you] immediately fall away." You have no staying power.

Or if you are the thorns that catch the seed, you're the "one who hears the word, but then worldly anxiety and the lure of riches choke the word and it bears no fruit." That applies to most of us—"anxiety... the lure of riches." We've all been there.

Whether you are the well-worn path, rocky ground, or thorny thicket—each offers resistance to the seed. Each of us has his or her own reason for resisting the seed. The Lord is calling upon us today through the words of this Gospel message to examine ourselves, to look into our lives, and to note—for no one's eyes but your own and God's—where the resistance lies to the seed of the Gospel that Christ is trying to plant in your life.

If we stop resisting and let it grow, what a difference it will make in our lives and in the life of the world. Who knows how much better you or your world would be? Christ knows and he's trying to tell you to expect a thirty, sixty, or a hundredfold improvement if only you give him the ground he needs to grow in your life.

47

Sixteenth Sunday of the Year

Wisdom 12:13; 16–19; Psalm 86; Romans 8:26–27;
Matthew 13:24–30

AN ENEMY HAS DONE THIS

It is always a challenge to preach at a Mass where there is a mix, as there is today, of adults and children—both interested in hearing the word of God. You don't want to ignore (or bore) the children while speaking only to the adults. Nor do you want to lose the adults by focusing exclusively on the children. It is interesting at times to try to listen through the others' ears—that is, for the elders to listen to God's word as proclaimed and explained to the youngsters, or for the young ones to listen through grown-up ears although, admittedly, that is not easily done. And there are times when it is important to preach adult themes to the adult audience even though that is done at the risk of losing the attention of the children. There is no one-size-fits-all solution.

Today, however, we have a story with a villain, and that might be something we can talk about together. There's an enemy in today's Gospel story; everyone knows what an enemy is. Is there anyone here who doesn't know what an enemy is? Is there anyone here who has never had an enemy?

Is there anyone here who doesn't know that Jesus gave us instruction—a commandment really—to love our enemies (even that brother or sister who is always hitting you and trying to do you in!)?

Let's go to the story, but I want to take a moment before I do to tell you something interesting that ran through my mind recently when I received news of the death of a Jesuit friend who died in New York City after a bout with cancer (cancer was his enemy, you might say). I

165

said to myself, "May God be good to him." And then I thought, that's a strange thing to say (or pray). How could God be anything but good to him? Think about that. An all-good God cannot be anything but good to us. We can harm ourselves, be bad to ourselves, if you will, by not letting God be good to us. But God can be nothing but good to all of us at all times.

That's kind of like a riddle, isn't it? And when you try to figure out that riddle, you are doing what theologians do, applying intellect to the mysteries of faith—trying to figure things out, trying to discover what God is like, attempting to get hold of a God who is always beyond our grasp.

In any case, let's go to the story. The Scripture refers to this story as a "parable." Does everybody know what a parable is? Parables have been described as extended similes (but to understand that you have to know what a simile is!). A simile is a comparison. It is a figure of speech in which two different things are compared by means of a "like" or an "as." A bicycle racer moves like lightning on his bike. A champion golfer's drive is like a cannon off the tee. School is like prison (no one here would ever say that!); summer camp is like heaven. You might say that something is as smooth as silk. You get the point. Similes are all about comparisons.

Well, a parable is an extended simile. It takes the comparison and stretches it out into a story. And Jesus does just that in this morning's Gospel story: "The kingdom of heaven may be likened to a man who sowed [that means planted] good seed in his field. While everyone was asleep his enemy came and sowed weeds all through the wheat, and then went off. When the crop grew and bore fruit, the weeds appeared as well. The slaves of the householder came to him and said, 'Master, did you not sow good seed in your field? Where have the weeds come from?' He answered, 'An enemy has done this.'"

And then, as you recall, his servants—his farmhands, really—asked if they should pull up the weeds. But he told them not to. He said wait until regular harvest time and then the wheat will have grown and can be separated from the weeds as both are removed from the field. To pull the weeds out prematurely would mean destroying the wheat as well.

Now remember, Jesus is telling you in this parable what the entrance into the kingdom of heaven is like. There are no "early admissions," so to speak, of the wheat not yet fully grown, nor are there early rejections for the killer weeds that were planted by an enemy. Both grow together and remain together until harvest time. The wheat has to learn how to get along in the world without being taken out by the weeds, without, you might say, permitting itself to give up on healthy growth and letting itself turn into weeds.

"An enemy has done this," the Gospel story says. Enemies are at work all over the world. We have enemies who attacked us on September 11, 2001. Computer users have to worry about unknown enemies who secretly try to inject a virus into another person's computer system. Technicians protect us from hackers. Police protect us from unknown enemies who might steal our property or harm our bodies. The armed forces are there to protect our nation from its enemies.

There are a lot of good people trying their best every day to do the right thing, and in that way they protect the common good. You can be part of that effort, being a good person doing the right thing and your efforts result in protection against the enemies of the common good.

Satan is an enemy who wants to destroy our souls. Other enemies line up against us. And what is our best line of defense? Well, take another look at the weeds and the wheat. Be careful not to tear right into the field and root everything up. If you do, you'll lose the wheat. Be calm. Be careful. Take the normal precautions to protect yourself and your property, just as we want our nation to take normal precautions to protect our borders, our airlines, our national symbols like the White House. Competence and vigilance are important parts of our personal and public defense strategies. It is important to remain calm and clear-minded. It is important to be alert and ready. And it is critically important, for the health of your soul, to remember that Jesus taught us to love our enemies. This doesn't mean like them any more than you like the weeds in your garden or lawns. But you have to love your enemies in the sense of hoping for their salvation, for their conversion from evil to good ways. To be consumed with hatred for another person who may indeed have done you wrong, is to tear up the weeds without thinking of the harm you are doing to the wheat, and ultimately to yourself!

Let me conclude by calling your attention to the words of today's Responsorial Psalm. It will help you all—the youngsters and the elders —to respond as Jesus would want you to respond to the story you have to consider in this morning's Gospel.

"Lord, you are good and forgiving, abounding in kindness to all who call upon you" (Ps 86:5). And so he is, the Lord your God is good and forgiving toward you. And the Lord invites you to be good and forgiving to others (even to your enemies). Just as they often say in sports that a "good defense is the best offense," your religious tradition says that your best defense against all your enemies is to be good and forgiving. Be alert too, of course, be on the alert at all times. But the busier you become in doing good, the stronger your defenses (both personal and national) will be against your enemies.

Think about this today and you'll find yourself thinking really deeply about what the kingdom of heaven is really like.

48

Seventeenth Sunday of the Year

1 Kings 3:5, 7–12; Psalm 119; Romans 8:28–30; Matthew 13:44–52

"ALL THINGS WORK FOR GOOD FOR THOSE WHO LOVE GOD"

The familiar and often-quoted sentence in today's reading from Paul's Letter to the Romans is both consoling and challenging. Listen to it once again: "We know that all things work for good for those who love God...." Indeed we do know that to be true, and we therefore find that verse to be enormously consoling when things go wrong—wrong, that is, from our earthbound point of view. But that sentence is also challenging. It could set the direction for a lifetime of theological reflection. Although we accept on faith this teaching of St. Paul, the saying itself is a challenge to our faith. It tests our faith. It invites us to a faith-based reflection on the meaning of life.

"We know that all things work for good for those who love God." I want to take you on an unusual route to a fuller appreciation of that truth. I want you, here in the midst of summer, to think of summers past. Recall good summer memories. Everyone has good early memories of summer. Being swept ashore with the surf, floating in an inner tube on a lake, splashing around in the pool, catching lightning bugs, chasing butterflies.

Memories recall Fourth of July fireworks, band concerts, baseball games, amusement parks, bike rides, roasted marshmallows, hamburgers and hotdogs, thunder and lightning, reading on the porch, sailing, waterskiing, summer jobs, hiking, and just hanging out. We tend to remember more readily what we came up with ourselves as "something to do," rather than the events that were organized for us. But we will always be grateful for those trips and family outings that we, in later life, take pains to provide for our own children and grandchildren.

Some parents inevitably find themselves asking, "Is it worth the hassle?" as they deplete their supply of patience and exhaust their peacemaking skills during long automobile trips that are part of the family vacation. Yes, it's worth it. The happy memories remain with those kids throughout their lives. How often do you hear them say, "D'ya remember when we…?" Yes, you certainly do, and so many of those are good summer memories.

Let yourself pray for a moment this morning in words like these:

Thank you, Lord, for summers past and summers yet to come.
Thanks for all the fun—fun with a purpose, like those great
    days at camp,
and fun for nothing else but the fun of it—in the attic,
    the backyard, the playgrounds,
the farms, the meadows, and the woods.
Thanks for summer rest, romance, and reflection.
There were summer moments, Lord, when you came
    toward me,
"walking on the waters," in a sense, as I felt your
presence in my life in summers past and caught a glimpse of
    your plan for me.
I've deviated from the plan, I know,
and I'm grateful for the mid-course corrections that
your providence provided for me from time to time.
Thank you also for the rains of summer, Lord, and
the growth-producing summer sun
that produced the summer crops and flowers and all things
    fresh.
Thanks for summer nights and summer sounds.
For love songs and for everything that summer sings to me now
by way of grateful thought and happy memory.

As I say, dear friends in Christ, you should let yourself pray. Let your summer thoughts feed your summer prayer. And after prayer, let your mind reflect on the truth of this saying: "We know that all things work for good for those who love God…" St. Paul completes that sentence with these words: "…who are called according to his purpose."

Think about that. All things work out for your good because you are "called according to his purpose." His purpose carries you out of the summer of your life into autumn, into the fall of life, and on into winter followed, of course, by spring. And there too, just as you see God's purpose in the seasons, you see God's purpose in your life. You see God working all things into good because he loves you and has called you to a life of purpose.

An edge of sadness accompanies an autumnal awareness of the passage of time and the fragility of life. Autumn without sunlight would be unimaginable. Autumn without rain would delay the return of those colder days that have been standing by, waiting for their annual reentry into our lives. Indian summer, that lovely span of warm afternoons that take us by surprise shortly after the first frost, lifts our spirits briefly before letting us gently down into the vestibule of winter. That, at least, is how I remember the change of seasons from summer to fall.

Autumn as a word may have a root relationship to words in other languages for increase or augment, as the crops increase to their harvest readiness in the season we call autumn. Much more likely, the word simply means autumnal, not autonomous, just autumnal— transitional from warm to cold. The human heart can find itself growing that way too. That's why the edge of sadness that comes with the autumn season, either in your year or in your life, cannot be left to grow beyond the dimensions of a hint or suggestion. Check it at the onset. Brush it off and look ahead with confidence. The best is yet to come.

For some of you this is the autumn of life. You know what is behind; you have no idea how much time there is to go. But this is nothing new. You've always been in transition. Your reach is always exceeding your grasp. Your soul is stretching out toward God. For some, you are in the winter season of life. You are clearly closer to the end than to the beginning. Faith tells you that you will pass through death to life, through winter to resurrection springtime.

You've been called according to God's purpose. Your life moves in cycles, like the seasons, and the seasons themselves suggest a purpose, a plan for you in God's creation. I guess what I'm attempting to do on this mid-summer Sunday is to stimulate your faith-based reflection on a comparison between yourself and the four seasons. You, like the seasons, pass through difficulties to delights, through downside losses to upside gains, through dark to light, from warmth to cold and back to warmth again. Behind your own ups and downs there is at work in you the principle Paul enunciates for you in today's reading from Romans: "We know that all things work for good for those who love God, who are called according to his purpose." Try to bring yourself for a moment this morning to say "Amen" to that!

You have, by God's grace, the "understanding heart" that Solomon requested of the Lord in this morning's first reading, and which, by the way, the Lord was happy to grant to both Solomon and to you. The Lord has given you a "wise and understanding heart." That heart enables you to recognize the kingdom of heaven for what it is—as explained to you by Jesus in the Gospel reading: like a treasure, like the pearl of great price.

Be prepared to sell all you have to purchase the land where that treasure lies buried. Be prepared to sell all that you have in order to buy that pearl of great price. And be ready to cast your net wherever the Lord prompts you to cast it and prepare yourself to bring in a great catch.

So just let yourself reflect this morning, let yourself become a mid-summer theologian and reflect on the truth that St. Paul puts before you: "We know that all things work for good for those who love God, who are called according to his purpose." And try to see God's purpose in the cycle of the seasons as well as in the seasons of your life.

49

Eighteenth Sunday of the Year

Isaiah 55:1–3; Psalm 145; Romans 8:35, 37–39; Matthew 14:13–21

"GIVE THEM SOME FOOD YOURSELVES"

The texts today provide us with an opportunity to talk about hunger—world hunger, chronic malnutrition—the kind of hunger that most of us will never know, but all of us can, if we determine to do it, help eliminate. Persons like you and me who have food, may have many problems. But a person who has no food is aware of only only one problem—hunger. Despite our many problems, we can, if we choose, address that one problem and eventually eliminate hunger from the face of the earth.

At Holy Trinity in Washington, DC, as you leave church each week, you pass under a sign that reminds you of the challenge of the judgment scene in Matthew 25: "Lord, when did we see you hungry?" On Monday mornings you go back to work on Capitol Hill, in the White House, in law firms, trade associations, lobbying organizations, or to other influential jobs around town where you might find yourself wondering how, from your workplace observation post, you can see and do something for the hungry poor. Those of you who are homemakers work, of course, even if you are not on a payroll. But you can also, along with retired persons, "get to work"—for the hungry poor by becoming part of the Christian citizens' lobby known as Bread for the World.

We are a Bread for the World "covenant church." We make a modest annual contribution. We have our "offering of letters" to Congress. Individual parishioners participate in a variety of ways. Fifteen or twenty of our parishioners have met occasionally here at the parish with Bread for the World President David Beckmann to offer strategy advice and enlist Congressional co-sponsors for legislation that BFW is trying to advance

173

on Capitol Hill. Our parishioners helped a lot one year with the "Africa: From Hunger to Harvest" resolution and, more recently, with the effort to help elected representatives see the moral urgency of changing for the better, so far as poor people in our country are concerned, the TANF program (Temporary Assistance for Needy Families).

According to a saying that used to make the rounds in Dorothy Day's Catholic Worker movement, "the trouble with the world is that the people who do all the thinking never act, and the people who do all the acting never think." In the face of worldwide hunger and poverty, a combination of thought and action powerful enough to deal with huge societal problems is particularly necessary. Where faith and works combine to shape both thought and action, provisioning strategies for the hungry poor of the world will emerge. Perhaps it will not happen in the way the solution you heard in today's Gospel story occurred, where Jesus, whose "heart was moved with pity" for a crowd of hungry people, said to his disciples, "There is no need for them to go away; give them some food yourselves." And as you know, the disciples said to him that all they had was five loaves and two fish. They didn't know what to do. So he took the loaves and fish and miraculously multiplied them so that everyone had enough to eat.

As you noticed, the disciples of Jesus in this story did not know what to do. So he intervened with a miracle. He had said to his disciples, "There is no need for them [the hungry] to go away [in search of food], give them some food yourselves." But the disciples did not know what to do. The same might be said of us today—disciples of Christ confronted with the problem of world hunger, but not knowing what to do.

Unless you are content simply to blame the victim, you have to look around for what might be causing the physical and emotional weariness of those who suffer hunger and poverty. You have to try to identify the source of the burdens that are crushing the powerless. If the causes remain unattended, the weariness and hunger will persist and the burdens will just grow heavier. Hunger is the most urgent form of poverty, and poverty can be defined simply as sustained deprivation. The question is then, of course, deprived of what? And sustained by what? Or by whom? Poverty is the root cause of hunger. What is sustaining the poverty, which, in turn, sustains the hunger?

The poor can't count on miracles. The hungry cannot eat promises. It is unlikely that angels will appear on the scene to ease their burdens. Humans helping humans is the way to go. Not the only way to go, say those who believe that miracles are indeed possible. But humans helping humans is a realistic way to go, given the fact that the "miracles" that happen in communities of good and faithful people seem to take a little longer these days.

Bread for the World's annual report one year bore the title, "Foreign Aid to End Hunger." It was able to predict the success of BFW's "Hunger to Harvest Resolution: A Decade of Concern for Africa." This was a concurrent House-Senate Resolution adopted by the Congress at the urging of Bread for the World. Through it, our nation went on record as wanting to increase effective aid to sub-Saharan Africa. This is not short-term food aid. It is not immediate relief. It is longer-term development assistance. We, as a nation, are committing ourselves to help poor countries build the infrastructure necessary for the production and transportation of food. The ultimate solution to hunger is the production of food in the food-deficit nations. And where food simply cannot be produced, it can be imported if appropriate trade and transportation arrangements are in place. All this, of course, presupposes political stability.

We here in the United States can practice both stewardship and citizenship by calling upon our representatives in government to do what we as a rich and powerful nation can do, namely, help poor countries to help themselves. This means debt relief and large injections of economic development assistance.

This is a "Moral Calling," says the BFW annual report for 2001:

Ending hunger is a moral calling. The most important arguments for increasing poverty-focused development assistance are moral. A sense of moral obligation provides the push (the 'ought'); and a vision of happy, healthy people ('the common good') provides the pull.

Moral sentiment rises partly from the realization that other people are just like us. When impoverished people get up in the morning they go through the same routines as people in the industrialized world—washing, eating, working, loving, and struggling. At night when they lie down, they too hope for a safe and secure tomorrow. In spite of cultural differences, we are all, ultimately, one human race.

So follow the public policy issues as well as the hunger and famine stories in the news. Let those for whom you vote know that you want development assistance and hunger reduction to be locked together in foreign policy. If you want more information, go to www.bread.org or locate Bread for the World in the phone book. Give them a call. Visit their offices.

Consider this kind of involvement to be your response to the direction Jesus gives in today's Gospel: "There is no need for them to go away; give them some food yourselves."

He came up with a miracle in his day. Our day calls for another kind of miracle called citizen participation. It takes a little longer, but it also provides a long-lasting solution.

50

Nineteenth Sunday of the Year

1 Kings 19:9, 11–13; Romans 9:1–5; Matthew 14:22–33

"WHY DID YOU DOUBT?"

Jesus asks a question in this morning's Gospel story that each one of us will ask ourselves from time to time—"Why did you falter?" It must always be asked upon examination after a lapse. It should be asked on occasion because, as everyone knows, the unexamined life is not worth living. So look at your lapses and ask: Why did I doubt?

In the Gospel account, the faltered attempt to walk on water took Peter down. Had Jesus not stretched out his hand to catch him, Peter would have sunk. But why did he falter? Why did he doubt? Apparently, it was his lack of faith. Walking on water is not a routine exercise. When you stop to examine the possibility carefully, doubts engulf you right away. Without faith, it can't be done.

Faith is a precondition of discipleship. It is a condition of entry into companionship with Jesus. You can't just sign up—get your membership card, so to speak—and join the club. No, you make a commitment from within; you align your will with what you believe to be the will of God for you, and you move forward on what can only be called a journey of faith.

That journey begins for most of us in infancy, at baptism; we are born Catholics. But there has to be a confirmation—a recommitment—somewhere along the line. For most of us, it is a sacramental confirmation early on. It could be an adult recommitment, a conscious reconnection with the Lord, a conscious choice to realign your will with that of God, to pattern your life on the life of Christ, to follow a path that is not always clear, to search for light that is not always there.

The journey of faith requires that you not be a passive participant, along for the ride. You've got choices to make about direction and destination, about speed and duration, about companions along the way. The journey of faith requires activity of you—human activity—activity of mind and heart; it requires acts of faith, and hope, and love.

The Sunday liturgy is a good setting to inquire about your faltering on the journey of faith. You hear God's word here. You gather with fellow believers around the table of the Lord. You remember your Lord in the breaking of the bread. You give thanks. You receive Eucharistic nourishment for the next stage of your journey of faith. You also have quiet moments to reflect on where that journey is taking you, which is to say, in what directions and distances your free choices will take you, as you continue to follow Christ in the week ahead.

Not all of us find God easily in the words from Scripture that are proclaimed in the Eucharistic assembly. Not all of us are sufficiently attentive when the word is proclaimed; not all are prepared to receive it. Not all of us show forth Christ adequately to one another as we gather around the altar; it is not always easy to locate Christ in our midst. You'll remember that Jesus said whenever two or three are gathered in my name, there I am in their midst. Well, it is sometime difficult to find Jesus here in our midst. Not all of us who stand at the altar in the person of Christ to offer this sacrifice—this re-presentation of the sacrifice of Calvary—not all of us priests measure up adequately to our representative responsibility. And although we surely—all of us—believe that Jesus is present during the sacrifice, truly present body and blood, soul and divinity under the appearance of bread and wine, we falter a bit in our watery walk of faith even here in the liturgy.

So let's return to the Gospel story for another moment. The story begins with Jesus insisting that his disciples pile into the boat; off they go as he slips away to pray before walking around to the other side of the lake where he will meet the boat at the shore. He remained alone to pray. About what? We have no way of knowing. We can assume that he prayed for them. We can even assume that he prayed for us. We just don't know. We do know that he united himself somehow—mind and heart—with his Father and their Holy Spirit.

The disciples huddled in the boat—what did they discuss? We don't know. We can assume that they talked a lot about the miracle they had witnessed—the multiplication of the loaves and fishes, the miraculous feeding of thousands of people. They had to wonder about the power of this Jesus whom they were following and about the future of the movement he was launching. They were part of that movement, but where was it going, where would they wind up.

The Gospel story indicates that a storm stirred up. I've been there at that lake in Israel. It is referred to in Scripture as the Sea of Galilee or the Lake of Tiberias; both names refer to the same body of water. It is located below sea level and thus subject to sudden temperature inversions with resulting high winds and stormy effects. The Gospel reading says: "Meanwhile, the boat, already a few miles offshore, was being tossed about by the waves, for the wind was against it. During the fourth watch of the night, he [Jesus] came toward them walking on the sea. When the disciples saw him walking on the sea, they were terrified. 'It is a ghost!' they said, and they cried out in fear. At once Jesus spoke to them: 'Take courage! It is I. Do not be afraid!' Peter said to him in reply, 'Lord, if it is you, command me to come to you on the water.'"

Notice the "if." There is doubt, not faith, in the midst of all the fright, but notice also that doubt does not disqualify you from the community of believers. And Jesus said, "Come!"

Peter got out of the boat and began to walk on the water toward Jesus [who was closer to shore.] But when he [Peter] saw how strong the wind was he became frightened; and beginning to sink, he cried out, "Lord, save me!" Immediately Jesus stretched out his hand and caught Peter, and said to him, "O you of little faith, why did you doubt?"

So here we are, back where we began. Why did you doubt? Jesus provided the answer before he asked the question: "How little faith you have!"

Those words apply to us, as we return to our liturgical remembrance, as we resume our respective journeys of faith. How little faith each one of us has. How much we depend on Jesus to encourage and instruct us, indeed to feed us with his sacred body and blood to keep us sure-footed and strong on our respective journeys of faith.

51

Twentieth Sunday of the Year

Isaiah 56:1, 6–7; Psalm 67; Romans 11:13–15, 29–32;
Matthew 15:21–28

THE CANAANITE WOMAN:
PERSISTENCE IN PRAYER

The Gospel story today provides you with a case study in persistence—persistence in prayer. And is there anyone among us who does not need that? We pray, but we pray sporadically and half-heartedly. We knock, but we don't keep on knocking; we ask, but we don't keep asking. We pray, but we are not persistent in prayer. Well, take another look at this Gospel story and you will learn that persistence pays off.

The Canaanite woman in this story is a mother. She has a daughter with a serious affliction. She knows that Jesus is a healer—indeed, he has performed miracles in full view of the people. So she approaches Jesus and explains to him her plight: "Have pity on me, Lord, Son of David! My daughter is tormented by a demon." But curiously, according to the Gospel story, Jesus "did not say a word in answer to her." He appears to have no pity all.

That is certainly strange. Apparently, Jesus is not only unresponsive, but rude to her. His disciples intervened and it is not clear whether they are asking him to do what she asks and thus "get rid of her," or whether they too want to ignore her. "She keeps calling out after us," they say to Jesus.

Persistence on her side; total stonewall unresponsiveness on the part of Jesus and his disciples.

This is a puzzling situation made all the more puzzling by the response Jesus gives to his disciples: "I was sent only to the lost sheep of the house of Israel." We know his mission was a lot wider than that.

He narrows the range of his responsiveness here for reasons that are not at all clear. In any case, he is ignoring the Canaanite woman's request. So the Gospel story goes on to say, "But the woman came forward and did him homage saying, 'Lord, help me!'" How many times have you said those exact same words in prayer? "Lord, help me!"

Whenever you do that you are making a prayer of petition. The answer will sometimes be "No" or "Not exactly as you ask," but your prayer will always be answered. That's why the reaction of Jesus in this Gospel story is so puzzling. To make matters worse, he tells her: "It is not right to take the food of children and throw it to the dogs." Not a very encouraging comment. But she, in her persistence, comes right back at him: "Please Lord, for even the dogs eat the scraps that fall from the table of their masters" Well, that seems to do it for Jesus. The Gospel goes on to say: "Jesus then said to her in reply, 'O woman, great is your faith! Let it be done for you as you wish.' And the woman's daughter was healed from that hour."

That's a great story. Let it serve both as a reminder and a tribute to the power of persistence in prayer.

The prayer of asking—prayer of petition, as it is often described—is not the sum and substance, beginning and end, be all and end all, of prayer. Not by any means. This is not to say that your prayer of petition is unimportant. It is simply to acknowledge that more advanced forms of prayer, contemplative prayer, for example, and other privileged ways of experiencing God, are available to us poor mortals. Indeed the Holy Spirit wants to pray *within* us, if only we say yes. Nonetheless, the prayer of petition is familiar and just about universal ("Give us this day our daily bread...").

"Gimme, gimme, gimme," is an immature and unsophisticated (even impolite) approach to anyone, let alone to God, your Creator and Lord. Still, God wants to hear from you. Sure, he knows your needs before you can articulate them. But in a wonderfully loving and mysterious way, God wants you to enlarge your capacity to receive more and more of his love by stretching out—enlarging—your need-filled soul through your prayers of petition. Ask, and you shall indeed receive. All too often, however, the prayer of petition is misunderstood and misapplied by the one who makes it.

Let me offer you an example that may help you better understand how the prayer of petition works. Reflect for a moment on your own personal experience on a lake, a bay, or river when you are in a boat drawing near to dock. Typically, you would throw a rope (a "line") toward the dock hoping to catch it on a permanent cleat. Once the line is caught on the cleat, you begin to pull. Notice that you are pulling yourself and your boat toward the dock, not the other way around. And yet how often do you toss your prayers of petition up to God, like lines going toward a dock, and immediately try to pull the dock (God) to you! You pray, in effect, for God's will to align itself with yours, for God to come to you, on your terms and conditions, when it should be exactly the other way around.

So, when you pray your prayer of petition—to get that job, make that sale, pass that exam, overcome that cancer, have a child restored to health—what you must do first is make yourself disposable and disposable to the will of a God who loves you more than you can imagine. Ask for whatever you want, but try to bring yourself to say that you want it *only if* God wants it for you.

Sometimes apparently, if anything is to be learned from today's Gospel message, God wants you to keep on asking. And as you keep on asking, you should remember the lesson in a wise prayer that comes from the lips of St. Thomas More: "The things, good Lord, that we pray for, give us the grace to labor for." In effect, the Lord's response to your prayer, a response that you may not be hearing, is: "Right, it's yours; you've just got some work to do—like studying, eating well, getting your exercise, making a few calls—to make sure it happens!"

So, be persistent in making your demands on God in prayer, but realize that God may also be making a few demands of you. Or, as seems to be the case with the Canaanite woman, God may want to hear from you just one more time!

52

Twenty-First Sunday of the Year

Isaiah: 22:15, 19–23; Psalm 138; Romans 11:33–36;
Matthew 16:13–20

"WHO DO YOU SAY THAT I AM?"

Jesus confronts you with a direct question in today's Gospel reading: "Who do you say that I am?" It's a fair question; one, perhaps, that the disciples did not expect, but fair nonetheless. They had been with him for more than a year, listening to him speaking to the crowds, observing him healing the sick and working miracles, piecing together elements of his plan to establish a kingdom of justice, peace, and love. They surely had some notion of who he was, so he asks them to make that notion explicit.

Some speak up and report what other people are saying—fair enough, because his initial question was "Who do people say that the Son of Man is?" And they replied by reporting what they had been hearing—John the Baptizer, Elijah, Jeremiah, or one of the prophets. There was indeed something prophetic about Jesus, not in the sense of foretelling the future but in the sense of authoritative statements about the present human condition and warnings that if present injustices went uncorrected, dire consequences would follow. Jesus was strong and outspoken, so it was natural for people to take him to be one of the prophets.

That's all very interesting, Jesus says to them, in effect, but what about you, who do you say that I am? He may have done this with some amusement, or he could have been deadly serious, going directly to the core issue of his identity since so much depended on their understanding of the nature of the enterprise he was launching—he was beginning a movement, establishing a community of believers eventually called Church that would represent him on earth, a community that would embody his person and presence with us on earth until the end of time. Not an insignificant question, therefore: "Who do you say that I am?"

Let me direct that question to each of you today. Who do you say that Jesus is—not was, but is—in your life, in your world today?

You might begin by saying that Jesus is Lord, that Jesus is divine, that Jesus is the Son of God and, as he liked to say, Son of Man, placing due emphasis on his humanity.

I like to think of Jesus as person and power. He is Lord, Creator and Redeemer, yes, but he is also friend, a personal friend. He knows me better than I know myself. He loves me to an extent that I can neither imagine nor appreciate. He is there for me—with me, by me—now and forever. I am a Christian; therefore I am never only me, I am never alone. And it is not just that I live in the company of other Christians; I live in the company of Christ. I am his companion. And thinking of him as I do, as person and power, I am linked to power; I can do all things, as St. Paul said, in him who strengthens me.

Rather than making me feel proud and arrogant, this estimate I have of who Jesus is makes me feel humble. The power is his, not mine, but our friendship gives me access to his power; it is available to me; it is at work in me. I have no reason at all to fear. Who do I say that he is? He is my security. Simple as that—he is there for me; I am secure, unworthy but secure.

Let this exercise roll out in your own minds now and later on today, perhaps, think this out with a pen or pencil in your hand. Write out your own answer to the question Jesus puts before you today: "Who do you say that I am?" It is a question you can but should not ignore and probably have been ignoring for quite a while. It is a question that opens the door to an exploration into God. Jesus is God, of course, but he is God in flesh—your flesh—he is like you in all things but sin. He knows your suffering; he knows your joy; he knows your fear; he knows your hope.

Notice also that this Gospel story gives special place to Peter. He is a leader of the apostles. He feels comfortable in speaking up. So when Jesus asks him to articulate his understanding of who Jesus is, Peter says flat out: "You are the Messiah, the Son of the living God." And this draws praise from Jesus. He compliments Peter. "Blest are you Simon, son of Jonah! For flesh and blood has not revealed this to you, but my heavenly Father." And then Jesus adds an ecclesial dimension to what is going on here, he puts his own personal identity into the context of the Church that he will establish and which Simon Peter will lead. "And so I say to you [Simon], you are Peter and upon this rock I will build my church, and the gates of the netherworld shall not prevail against it. I will give you the keys to the kingdom of heaven. Whatever you bind on earth shall be bound in heaven; whatever you loose on earth shall be loosed in heaven."

This extraordinary power—his power, the power of the keys—is given by Jesus to his Church under the leadership of Peter. The power to bind and loose, to free or condemn. This is simply extraordinary. So much so that if you reconsider the question "Who do you say that I am?" you now have to include an ecclesial dimension in your reply. Yes, he is the Messiah. Yes, he is the Son of God and Son of Man. Yes, he is person, power, friend, but he is also in some mysterious way Church. No longer can we think of Jesus apart from his Church. The Church is where you find him. The Church is where he is at work in our world. He is at work through the sacraments of the Church, for example; he speaks to us through the voice of the Church. His identity is Church; the Church is he.

Remarkable. Extraordinary. So much to consider, to ponder. So much to consolidate into your reply to the question he puts before you today, "Who do you say that I am?"

Don't be sorry that he asked the question. Just be sorry—for yourself—if you are unwilling to face up to a complete answer to his question. The implications of that answer touch you now where you are here on earth and stretch out to where we hope you and all of us with you will be forever in eternity.

53

Twenty-Second Sunday of the Year

Jeremiah 20:7–9; Psalm 63; Romans 12:1–2; Matthew 16:21–27

WHOEVER LOSES HIS OR HER LIFE
FOR MY SAKE WILL FIND IT

Labor Day 2002 fell just nine days before the first anniversary of the terrorist attacks on the Twin Towers and the Pentagon. Those who lost their lives that day were working people. They were on the job when they died. We can honor their memory by prayerful reflection this Labor Day Weekend about the value of work and the worth of workers.

"*Laborare est Orare*," is the Benedictine maxim. "To work is to pray." That applies to all believers in or out of the Benedictine tradition. As Labor Day approaches, recall that the victims of 9/11 departed this world from their workplace oratories.

Workers deserve our prayers this weekend. Simple justice calls for a prayer of gratitude for those whose labors give us what we need to sustain and enjoy life. Workers, organized and unorganized, skilled and unskilled, employed and unemployed, deserve a place in our Labor Day prayers.

If you have others working for you, ask yourself if you ever pray for them—for their health, happiness, and eternal salvation. If that notion strikes you as quaint, take it as a measure of the gap between matter and spirit in your life. The spiritual should indeed matter to you. But it won't count for much if you make no room for it in practical areas like the world of work.

The "world of work" is a worthy subject of prayerful reflection. Work is God's gift to us, a means by which we realize our potential and give our talents a good stretch. Work is the way we serve one another (and thus show our love for one another). Those who fall behind or are left out of the world of work stand in need of prayer in their struggle to get back on track. Pray for them on Labor Day.

There is more to life than work, of course. There is more to any worker than the function he or she performs. We are human beings not human doings. We have to guard against defining ourselves or anyone else in terms of what we do. We especially have to guard against the great American secular heresy that what you do is what you are, and when you "do nothing" (are unemployed or in retirement) you are nothing. So much self-esteem has been crushed under the weight of that false conclusion!

Pity anyone who views low-skill or menial work as unimportant and those who perform it as "nothings."

I know of a business school professor who puts the following question on his mid-term examination: "What is the name of the worker who cleans this classroom and the corridor outside?" His response to the howls of protest from angry students: "I'm just preparing you to become a good employer. If you don't know the little people by name, you won't be providing good leadership in your organization. And if you think the question was unfair, I'll make it up to you by telling you now that the same question will be on the final exam!"

On Labor Day think about the work you do. Be grateful for all the gifts that enable you to do it. Think about the workers who stand behind so many of the products and services that you tend to take for granted. Think of those who are unemployed or on the margins of the workforce in low-paying jobs. Well beyond our borders are those who are trapped between misery and workplace exploitation. Labor Day prayer might open up the question of what we can do to make the world of work a better place for all of them.

Now take these reflections and hold them up against the words Jesus spoke to you in today's Gospel selection: "Whoever wishes to come after me must deny himself, take up his cross and follow me. For whoever wishes to save his life will lose it, but whoever loses his life for my sake will find it." How does the work you do relate to that? Is there anything in this Gospel passage to think about on Labor Day?

Jesus continues: "What profit would there be for one to gain the whole world and forfeit his life [earlier translations used to say: "forfeit or lose his soul]? Or what can one give in exchange for his life [for his or her soul]?" This is the famous passage associated with Ignatius of Loyola and Francis Xavier when both were students at the University of Paris. Ignatius, seeing the potential in the young scholar-athlete Francis Xavier, put that question before him we are told. "Think about it, Francis," Ignatius would say, "What does it profit a man to gain the whole world and suffer the loss of his soul?" Ignatius wanted Francis to consider becoming a Jesuit. That question is before us now; it is there for us to consider when we think about work, careers, promotions, salaries, bonuses, job titles, workplace recognition. What does your work have to do with eternity? Let me assure you it has a lot to do with the bigger picture, with saving your soul, with making your contribution to a better world.

You spend so much of your time, so many of your waking hours on the job, at work, earning a living. Curious expression, isn't it, "Earning a living"? Life is a gift; we can't earn it. It's what you do with your life that makes the difference. Your earning facilitates your living, supports it, as we say, but you work to live; you surely should not permit yourself to live to work. You have to avoid the trap of being consumed by your job. And you certainly want to avoid working only to accumulate wealth.

We Christians are called to deny ourselves. Whoever of us wishes to save his or her life, will lose it, but whoever among us is willing to let go, be detached, refuse to be possessed by our possessions, whoever is willing for the sake of Jesus and his kingdom to lose his or her life, will find it. And this applies to the world of work; it applies to your attitude about work; to your gratitude for work; to your ability to give your talents a good stretch at work and to use the fruits of your labor. And it applies to the gain you take away from the workplace, not selfishly for your personal prestige, profit, and glory, but for the glory of God and the service of your brothers and sisters in the human community.

So these are a few things to reflect about over the Labor Day weekend. Be sure to think about trade unions too, ask God's blessing on them and their leaders. Notice that wherever in the world you have free trade unions, you do not have totalitarian rule.

Be grateful on Labor Day for the gift of work in your own life and for the contributions of workers to your personal and national well-being. See yourself in solidarity with other working people around the world. And remember that those who died so suddenly on September 11, 2001, left this world from their workplaces. When you return to your workplace, recall the Benedictine dictum *"Laborare est Orare"* and think of that workplace as your oratory where your labor gives praise and thanks to God.

54

Twenty-Third Sunday of the Year

Ezekiel 33:7–9; Psalm 95; Romans 13:8–10; Matthew 18:15–20

"WHERE TWO OR THREE ARE GATHERED TOGETHER IN MY NAME, THERE AM I IN THE MIDST OF THEM"

The closing sentence from today's Gospel reading, the selection you just heard from Matthew's Gospel, is both comforting and challenging. "Where two or three are gathered together in my name," says Jesus, "there am I in the midst of them."

We are gathered in his name. So, here he is in our midst. Where? Here. Right here among us. Now, you might be accustomed to thinking that Jesus is present in the tabernacle, in the consecrated bread that is "reserved" in the tabernacle for our adoration and devotion. He is, of course, present there; we sometimes speak of it as the "real presence." But the words you just heard from Matthew's Gospel are saying something else. Jesus is saying that he is present within and among us—yes, us! He is here in our midst. That doesn't necessarily mean in the middle of this congregation. He is there, of course, but he is out there on the sides; he is in the back and again up front. He is here wherever we are; he is in our midst.

He is easier to find among us if those of us who are gathered there who have smiles on our faces, kind words on our lips, and love in our hearts. If we are present to one another in that way, it is possible, even easy, for us to see Christ present there. He makes his presence felt through love, and we experience love from one another.

The second reading, the selection from Paul's Letter to the Romans, helps you navigate this reality and figure it out; it helps you understand love as the indicator of our purpose and identity as Christians. Paul instructs us to "owe nothing to anyone except to love one another." Nice to be debt-free in our economic dealings, but we can never be debt-free in our religious and spiritual lives. We are bound to love one another and we can never discharge that debt completely because there are always others around us. No one of us is an island. We are persons, yes, but we are also a people of God. We are all in this together. There are always others whom we must love.

We live, as Paul reminded the Romans, under familiar commandments of the law covering adultery, murder, stealing, and covetousness. But all the commandments of the law, says Paul, are summed up in this: "You shall love your neighbor as yourself." And he adds: "Love does no evil to the neighbor; hence, love is the fulfillment of the law."

So look around and see those you are commanded to love. Hard to love them, if you don't know them, you might find yourself saying. But you get the idea. You live under a commandment of love. And if you observe that commandment—if you do indeed love one another—Jesus, as promised, is there in your midst whenever you gather, as you are gathered at this moment, in his name.

This is an important dimension of what we traditionally call our "Sunday obligation." We are obliged to be here, but that obligation becomes no burden, no debt at all if we create a warm, welcoming environment of love for one another. Our church architecture and furniture arrangements are not always conducive to that open environment. Sometimes we can neither see not hear one another. We get a good look at the backs of other people's heads as we celebrate the Eucharist; we enter and exit the worship space without a greeting or good-bye to fellow worshippers. We are unsmiling as we come and go; we are uncommunicative as we form a gathered assembly. And yet, if we are to take Jesus at his word, he is here in our midst. So we might give some thought to simple ways in which we can permit him to make his presence better known—through us.

The Gospel reading gets at some of those bothersome things that crop up from time to time in human communities. Your brother might commit some wrong against you. You may, on occasion, feel compelled to "tell him his [or her] fault." And in a quasi-arbitration, you might have to "take one or two others along with you, so that every fact may be established on the testimony of two or three witnesses." There's a role for the Church in such disputes. And extending this to what we might call "confessional matter," Jesus here again makes the extraordinary promise to back up what his Church, through its sacramental system, binds or looses. "I assure you," says Jesus, "whatever you declare bound on earth shall be held bound in heaven, and whatever you declare to be loosed on earth shall be loosed in heaven."

And the Gospel message doesn't stop there, It goes on to convey the extraordinary promise of Jesus that whenever we gather in his name—even just two or three of us—and agree to pray for anything whatever, "it shall be granted to them by my heavenly Father." Your reaction to that may be a bit skeptical. That's understandable. But let your skepticism prompt you to examine the level of love in your community of two or three from which that prayer emerges. Let it prompt you as well to examine the extent the presence of Jesus is seen and felt—yes felt—in your worshipping community. And give some thought also not only to what it is you are praying for, but to the possibility that the answer to your prayer might have been "No"—a gentle, loving refusal, but a refusal nonetheless. It might have been a "No, not yet," and that means you have to keep on praying. It could have been a "No, what you are asking for is not what I want you to be or have; it is not aligned with my will for you." And you simply have to accept that. In fact, any prayer of petition you make should be conditioned by a "not my will, but thy will be done—I want only what you want for me, what you know to be best for me!"

In any case, your takeaway from today's Gospel reading is both clear and compelling: "Where two or three are gathered together in my name, there am I in the midst of them." Think about that!

55

Twenty-Fourth Sunday of the Year

Sirach 27:30—28:7; Psalm 103; Romans 14:7–9;
Matthew 18:21–35

Contextual note: This homily was delivered a few days after the first anniversary of the September 11, 2001, terrorist attacks on the Twin Towers and the Pentagon.

HOW OFTEN MUST I FORGIVE?

For as the heavens are high above the earth,
so surpassing is his kindness toward those who fear him.
As far as the east is from the west,
So far has he put our transgressions from us.

These words, taken from the 103rd psalm, outline the dimensions of God's mercy. How great is it? As high as the heavens are above the earth, as wide as the east is from the west. These are the dimensions of God's forgiveness. Savor the words. Let them give you peace of heart. Let them fill your soul with trust. Be grateful for the forgiveness you have received. That's why you are here today, to give thanks for the forgiveness God has given you.

In today's Gospel, Peter asks Jesus: "Lord, if my brother sins against me, how often must I forgive?" Jesus replies in multiples—"not seven times but seventy-seven times." And then Jesus tells a story about a generous master who is "moved with compassion" and forgives a servant's loan. But the one whose obligation to repay was forgiven, himself becomes a creditor and refuses to forgive his fellow servant who happens to owe him money. On hearing of his hard-heartedness, his refusal to forgive, his master turns him over to torturers, and Jesus, who is telling this story, says to all of us who will hear it down through the centuries, "So will my heavenly Father do to you, unless each of you forgives your brother from your heart."

This is serious and demanding doctrine. Whoever said that being a Christian, a follower of Christ, a believer in Christ, was going to be easy? One of the first lessons you have to learn and put into practice, if you are going to be a good Christian, is the lesson of forgiveness. Is it possible that hidden somewhere in your heart or mind today is a block, a boulder, a weight that can be nothing else but a refusal to forgive? Is the pull of evil at work within us today, holding us back from forgiving others as we have been forgiven?

Let me invite you today to take a visual walk with me along the Way of the Cross. You see the Stations on the walls of your church. You see Jesus condemned to death. You see him shouldering the cross, falling, being stripped, scourged, nailed to the cross and hung there to die. There are indeed three stations of consolation: Veronica wipes his face; Simon of Cyrene helps to carry the cross; he finds his mother Mary standing there at the foot of the cross. But there he is unjustly condemned, hanging on the cross, suffering, waiting to die. And a soldier pierces his side with a lance. Blood and water flow out—symbols of baptism and the Eucharist, sacraments of life and reconciliation.

Now let me invite you to return to the images of September 11, 2001. They are etched in your memory. Imagine, if you will, a way of the cross that leads you to the Twin Towers and another that leads to the Pentagon. Not that these architectural symbols of wealth and power are to be viewed as standing in, as it were, for the body of Christ. But the people within those structures on the morning of September 11, 2001, were indeed the body of Christ. Those two buildings were gashed and wounded, and the people within them were killed. And imagine now, if you will, as you recall the picture of Ground Zero and "The Pit" that remained after the ruins were cleared, and recall also the gash in the side of the Pentagon after the crash, imagine that from those wounds the victim's blood and water flowed out of a pierced side, out of the body of Christ. And believe that from their death a new life might rise, just as resurrection followed the death of Jesus on the cross.

While you have the picture of Jesus there in your mind's eye, the crucified, crushed Jesus hanging on the cross, listen again to his words, what we call in our Good Friday devotions the "Seven Last Words" of Jesus on the cross. And notice that the first of these seven legacy messages from Jesus to us is this: "Father forgive them, they know not what they do" (Luke 23:34). And you say you cannot forgive your brother, or your sister, or your parents, or anyone else? And you say you cannot forgive the terrorists? "Father forgive them, they know not what they do."

And Jesus also said from the cross: "Amen, I say to you, today you shall be with me in Paradise." (Luke 23:43) Let yourself hear these words as addressed to you. Imagine that the thousands who died on September 11, 2001, heard these words addressed to them. Can you imagine Jesus refusing to say these words to those who perpetrated this evil? Perhaps you can. Perhaps he did. But what then becomes of the prayer, "Forgive them for they know not what they do?"

If you are struggling with forgiveness, turn to Mary. See her there at the foot of the cross. Hear him commend her to you and you to her: "Woman behold your son, your daughter," and hear him say to you: "Behold your mother" (John 19:26–27). Mary can help you.

If you are down—depressed, discouraged, afraid—make his words your own and just wait in silence for God's answer: "My God, My God why have you forsaken me?" (Matthew 27:46).

"I thirst" (John 19:30) said Jesus from the cross. Now, in the aftermath of terrorist attacks, you and I have to thirst for justice and do what we can to bring it about. Promotion of justice is the best possible way to prevent terrorism.

"It is finished" (John 19:30) said Jesus as his last moment drew near. Then he expired. "Father, into your hands I commend my spirit" (Luke 23:46). His expiration was literally a handing over of his Holy Spirit to us. He died that we might live. And as we live our lives today in the face of possible danger, with some awareness of uncertainty, troubled perhaps with a touch of anxiety, we commend ourselves, body and soul, to the Father. We trust in him and in his love for us. Let this trust work its way down into the very depths of your being.

And remember this. The forgiveness God offers you has dimensions that you can imagine by seeing how high the sky is above the earth, and how far the east is from the west. And remember too that unpleasant prospects await you "unless each of you forgives your brother from your heart."

56

Twenty-Fifth Sunday of the Year

Isaiah 55:6–9; Psalm 145; Philippians 1:20–24, 27; Matthew 20:1–16

A FAIR DAY'S PAY

This Gospel story is a puzzler for many people. Jesus speaks approvingly of an owner of a vineyard who has what appears to be strange hiring and payment policies, and Jesus compares that vineyard and its personnel polices with the way things are in the kingdom of God where, he says, "the last will be first and the first will be last."

The first reading from the Prophet Isaiah might help you create a context within which you can receive this curious Gospel lesson. Isaiah, as you will recall, urges his hearers to "turn to the Lord for mercy; to our God who is generous in forgiving." Generosity is the context, the framework for today's Gospel message. And Isaiah sketches out the dimensions of God's generosity: "As high as the heavens are above the earth, so high are my ways above your ways and my thoughts above your thoughts." That first reading is a useful benchmark in establishing the context for what Jesus is trying to teach in this story about the vineyard.

The owner of the vineyard goes out at dawn, hires some workers, and tells them that they will receive the usual daily wage. He goes out again at mid-morning and finds idle men in need of work, so he hires them and tells them they will be paid "whatever is fair." Again at noon time and in mid-afternoon, the owner goes out, finds still more un-hired hands, puts them to work and makes the same promise of a fair wage. It all sounds good and everyone seems to be happy.

"When it was evening, the owner of the vineyard said to his foreman, 'Summon the laborers and give them their pay.'" To the delight of those who were hired late (and the chagrin of those who began working at dawn), those hired last received a full day's pay, as did those who were the first to be hired. The promise of a "usual daily wage," a fair day's pay, was made to all; and that's what all received. The pay was equal but the length of time spent in the vineyard differed considerably. Those who were hired first and carried the full heat of the day complained, and most of us can relate to that. But the owner said to them, in effect, "Are you knocking me because I'm generous? You received what I promised to pay you; it was the amount you agreed to when I hired you. Take it and go home." And he went on to say, as any entrepreneur might say today, "[A]m I not free to do as I wish with my own money?" Well maybe so, maybe not; it depends on what he wants to do with that money. Then Jesus tacks on the lesson that we now have to consider, "Thus the last will be first and the first will be last."

The meaning of that saying is not immediately evident. Neither law nor logic require that the last be first and the first be last. The only way of understanding that is to put it in the context of generosity, divine generosity. We have an opportunity today to use this story as a reminder that we have a very big God. Our God is an unknown God, some might say, but that is not to concede that God is altogether unknowable. Jesus himself is a revelation of who God is, and what God is like. The teachings of Jesus help explain the nature of God. Here he is teaching us something about generosity and we can allow this teaching to help us become better informed on the important point of what God is like; we can also take this teaching as an instruction on how we, as followers of Jesus, should act in our daily lives. We can make Christ more fully present in our world by being generous. We can do God's will on earth by being generous to one another. The greater our generosity, the fuller the presence of Christ in our midst.

There are some lessons here in this story of vineyard personnel policies that Jesus surely approved. We can carry these lessons with us into our own lives and respective workplaces.

Some years ago, I met monthly with a group of business men and women—mostly Catholic, virtually all of them Christian—who wanted to explore the relevance of their religious faith to their daily task of meeting business responsibilities. We typically opened our meetings with a reading from Scripture, followed by five minutes of silent reflection and then an open-ended conversation on points prompted by the reading. On one occasion, we used the text that is our Gospel for today, the story of the owner of the vineyard promising to pay his workers what is fair. We had a lively discussion with active participation from the head of a large construction company, the president of a bank, and other veterans of many discussion of wage policy in the real world of business.

When we met again one month later, the banker told the group, "You won't believe what happened to me just a couple of days after we had that discussion last month about wage policy. My head of human resources came in to see me and said that he was getting concerned about the widening gap between entry-level compensation and executive-level compensation at the bank." Our discussion-group member said he viewed the compensation gap at his bank as a justice issue and he told us that his immediate response to the problem, when presented by his HR person, was to go back to the conversation he had had with the others about what religious faith requires of us in the workplace relative to a fair day's pay.

The entry-level compensation was too low, he decided; the executive level was more than adequate. Raise the entry level and hold the executive level was his way of translating the generous vineyard personnel policy found in Scripture into a working guideline for his own modern business, his way of closing the gap noticed by his human resources officer.

Let me suggest that you insert yourself into this Gospel story now. Insert yourself wherever you like—become the owner, the laborer hired at dawn, the fellow who was hanging around until mid-afternoon and then went to work. From whichever perspective you adopt, what is your reaction to the policy of generosity you observe here?

Now with a better understanding of the dimensions of God's mercy and generosity, apply God's generosity to yourself; notice how much you are a true beneficiary of that generosity. You can also apply the ethic of generosity, as you find it in this story, and put it to work in your immediate surroundings at home and work. That would be a worthy outcome of this reflection. That would be an excellent way to react to the puzzling story of the first being last and the last being first. Puzzle it out for yourself and give thanks to God for his great generosity to you.

57

Twenty-Sixth Sunday of the Year

Ezekiel 18:25–28; Psalm 25; Philippians 2:1–11; Matthew 21:28–32

ATTITUDE

This morning's second reading, a selection from Paul's Letter to the Philippians, invites you to "have in you the same attitude that is also in Christ Jesus." Think for a few moments now about attitude in general, and then reflect on sharing, internalizing, if you will, the attitude that was and is in Christ Jesus.

Some of you will remember February 20, 1962, when America's pioneer astronaut John Glenn blasted into orbit as part of the space race between the United States and the Soviet Union. We were behind in that race and John Glenn's success in orbiting the earth three times on that sunny day decades ago did much to restore American prestige worldwide as well as advance our progress in space exploration.

Glenn's Mercury spacecraft was named "Friendship 7." In it, John Glenn risked his life as he traveled at 17,500 miles per hour 160 miles above Earth. His autopilot function failed and he had to pilot the spacecraft manually. The world watched on television and listened to Mission Control wonder aloud whether the space capsule's heat shield would hold while reentering the earth's atmosphere, because, as the spacecraft began its second orbit, Mission Control received a signal that the heat shield was loose. Its function, as you know, was to prevent the capsule from burning up during reentry. Normally the retropacket package would be jettisoned after the rockets were fired to slow the capsule for reentry, In this case, however, Glenn was ordered to retain the retropack to hold the heat shield in place. As he struggled to maintain control of the spacecraft, John Glenn watched as huge chunks flew past the window and he wondered whether it was the retropack or the heat shield breaking up. The world held its breath at reentry time. The heat shield held. If it hadn't, John Glenn and his capsule would have been incinerated.

During those tense moments of flight maneuvers and instruction, the word "attitude" was frequently used by Mission Control—referring to the attitude of the space craft. I was intrigued by that vocabulary and soon realized, of course, that they were talking about the tilt, the direction of incline, the bias, the position of the capsule. It had to be tilted so that the heat shield would be there, if indeed it was still attached to the spacecraft, to make first contact with Earth's atmosphere. It was there. It held. John Glenn lived to tell the story of the flight. History was made. The mission was a success.

"Have in you the same attitude that is also in Christ Jesus." Paul is inviting you today to have a tilt, a bias, a direction, an attitude. Your tilt cannot be simply a nod or salute to Christ Jesus. More is required of the Christian than a membership card. There has to be commitment to the values of Jesus, a fidelity in following his way, a willingness to imitate him, to internalize his world view, to adopt his convictions, to make them your own, to internalize them. In other words, with the controls of your own life in your own hands (manual control, no autopilot), you have to tilt your life as Jesus tilted his. And what was his tilt, his bias, his attitude? Paul outlines it for you: "[T]hough he was in the form of God, [Jesus] did not regard equality with God something to be grasped. Rather, he emptied himself, taking the form of a slave coming in human likeness; and found human in appearance, he humbled himself, becoming obedient to the point of death, even death on a cross."

But Paul is quick to add: "Because of this, God greatly exalted him and bestowed on him the name that is above every other name."

Notice that he "emptied" himself. The Greek word for that is *kenosis* and the voluntary emptying out of power and glory on the part of Jesus in order to take our flesh and become like us so that he could save us, is sometimes call a "kenotic gesture." He didn't cling to his equality with God as a miser clings to his booty; no, he let go, he emptied himself. "Found human in appearance, he humbled himself" says Paul of Jesus. We have to think of ourselves in those terms. Are we sufficiently humble to live a "poured-out life," as Jesus did? He valued humility. He committed himself to a personal emptying out. Where are our values? What are our commitments?

A NASA news release in 2002 announced that something called the Global Positioning System is now "determining the attitude, position and speed of the International Space Station. This is the first successful use of GPS data in attitude control of a spacecraft, NASA officials and scientists believe. It is working well, feeding information on the station's attitude to systems that control its orientation in space. GPS also is providing more precise speed and position data than had been available. 'As far as I know, no one else is using GPS operationally for attitude determination,' said the Johnson Space Center's Susan Gomez," chief engineer of the Space Integrated Global Position System/Inertial Navigation System.

Here on earth, as our feet of clay try to find their way on the journey of faith, the word of God, preserved for us in the books of the Bible, should function as a "positioning system," an attitude setter. You have to take Sacred Scripture seriously. Whether you imagine yourself to be in a capsule or a canoe in your journey of faith, you can slip off course. You can tilt in the wrong direction. You can find yourself on a sharp incline that can let you slide away from God. You can cultivate biases (or permit a secular culture to cultivate them for you) that run counter to the biases that were part of the attitude that Jesus cultivated for himself and wants to share with you.

Today's selection from Philippians is just one of many readings that you can factor into your personal (as opposed to global) "positioning system." There is one I like from a secular, non-Christian source that echoes it and can function within your personal positioning system. It is from Mahatma Gandhi who said: "There comes a time when an individual becomes irresistible and his action becomes all pervasive in its effect. This comes when he reduces himself to zero." Another way of describing the kenotic gesture.

Look around for your own way of living the poured-out life, of emptying yourself out for others. And don't mistake this for doormat spirituality because the upside for you, as it was for Jesus, is also articulated by Paul in the text we've been considering: "Because of this, God greatly exalted him and bestowed on him the name which is above every name, that at the name of Jesus every knee should bend, of those in heaven and on earth and under the earth, and every tongue confess that Jesus Christ is Lord, to the glory of God the Father."

You can't expect any bended knees before you, but you can bet your life on the glory that awaits you in Christ Jesus your Lord if you make his attitude your own.

58

Twenty-Seventh Sunday of the Year

Isaiah 5:1–7; Psalm 80; Philippians 4:6–9; Matthew 21:33–43

HAVE NO ANXIETY AT ALL

Listen again to the words you heard proclaimed in this morning's second reading, the selection from St. Paul's Letter to the Philippians: "Have no anxiety at all, but in everything, by prayer and petition, with thanksgiving, make your requests known to God. Then the peace of God that surpasses all understanding will guard your hearts and minds in Christ Jesus."

"Have no anxiety at all." Sharpshooting, sniper killers were on the loose around the Washington Beltway in 2002 when I first delivered this homily. Talk about going to war in Iraq was heard all around town. West Nile virus was then a threat. Terrorist attacks were a distinct possibility. And Scripture was saying, "Have no anxiety."

The real world we inhabited then and now is not a safe place. Nine-eleven is nobody's lucky number. How can we not be anxious?

This gem of a sentence from Paul's Letter to the Philippians provides a prescription for anxiety. "In everything," Paul writes, "by prayer and petition, with thanksgiving, make your requests known to God." Note the prescribed steps: (1) prayer and petition; (2) thanksgiving; (3) make your requests known to God. Take these three steps and what can you expect? "Then the peace of God that surpasses all understanding will guard your hearts and minds in Christ Jesus." Believe it. Try it.

First, prayer and petition. Do you pray? Do you set aside some time each day for prayer? Do you understand prayer in a broader and far wider sense than just "Gimme, gimme, gimme; I want this; I need that"? Do you ever think of prayer as just being with, thinking about, listening to a personal God, a God who knows you, loves you, cares for you, holds your destiny in his hands the way so many of you have held an infant in your hands? Do you ever think of prayer as letting go, as just trusting—letting yourself fall into the arms of God; trusting and entrusting yourself to God's providence?

Yes, Paul says "prayer and petition." It is surely OK to ask, to plead, to make your petitions known and even to enlist the aid of the angels and saints, and Our Lady as well, in making your petitions known to your all-loving, all-powerful God. Ask God for safety and security for yourself and your loved ones. Ask God to protect our country. Ask God to lead us along the path to peace and away from war. Ask, ask, ask, and never tire of asking, but in the asking let yourself be drawn to God in a trusting relationship. Trust God enough to make all of your prayers of petition conditional prayers; condition them on God's will for you. "Not my will, but yours be done, O Lord." "Lord, only if it is your will for me," let me have this, that, or whatever else I find myself praying for.

The second step in Paul's prescription for the anxious is thanksgiving. "But in everything, by prayer and petition, with thanksgiving, make your requests known to God." Ingratitude will get you nowhere. Begin every prayer with a word of gratitude. Gratitude is the foundation, the infrastructure, the root of all religious experience. Gratitude also leads to a sense of moral obligation. Did you ever hear anyone say, "Much obliged," as an expression of gratitude, as a way of saying thanks? When you say "Thank you" to God; when you express your gratitude to God (which should be a daily occurrence in your life), you are declaring yourself to be "much obliged." Much obliged to continue giving thanks, to make your life an ongoing expression of gratitude, and to do good things for others because so many good things have come your way in God's gracious providence.

And point three in Paul's prescription is a repetition of the first: "make your requests known to God." "Haven't heard from you lately," God might say if you got a call from him today. Perhaps you are stewing in your own anxiety, too self-enclosed, too worried to even think about looking outward and upward to God. Too busy worrying to make your requests known to the only One who can put your worries to rest.

So, you've taken these three steps, then what? Paul says: "Then the peace of God that surpasses all understanding will guard your hearts and minds in Christ Jesus." Who could ask for anything more?

This prescription against anxiety is a formula for balance in your life. The Christian character is a balanced character. The balanced life is a peaceful life, a tranquil life. This is the life God wants each one of you to enjoy.

I want to remind you that this is Respect Life Sunday in our Archdiocese. Be grateful for the gift of the life that is yours. Have nothing but the profoundest respect for life wherever you encounter it. The Church teaches you to respect life from the moment of conception to the moment of natural death, and to do nothing that will harm or attack innocent human life. Keep that in mind as you think about the possibility of war in Iraq. Make respect for life your rule of life and you will have reduced significantly the complications that might otherwise introduce anxiety to your own life.

This is also Volunteer Sunday in our parish. Visit the volunteer fair after Mass and consider how volunteering might help to get you out of yourself and into the life of another who needs your help. As volunteer activity goes up, anxiety in the life of the volunteer goes down.

And finally, the Little Sisters of the Poor are here this Sunday asking for financial assistance, not for themselves, but for the frail elderly whom they serve with loving care. This parish is always generous to these gracious ladies; please give them a greenback greeting when you see them at the doors after Mass.

"Brothers and Sisters, have no anxiety at all, but in everything, by prayer and petition, with thanksgiving, make your requests known to God. Then the peace of God that surpasses all understanding will guard your hearts and minds in Christ Jesus."

To these reassuring words, we all can say "Amen!"

59

Twenty-Eighth Sunday of the Year

Isaiah 25:6–10a; Psalm 23; Philippians 4:12–14, 19–20;
Matthew 22:1–14

Contextual note: This homily was delivered in Washington, DC,
on a Sunday in October 2002, when an armed gunman—the
"Beltway sniper" was at large and shooting at cars in the Wash-
ington-area suburbs.

I CAN DO ALL THINGS IN HIM
WHO STRENGTHENS ME

These are days that are trying the hearts and souls, the minds and ner-
vous systems of people like you and me throughout the Washington
metropolitan area. We are forced to reflect on the fragility of life. We
are slammed right up against the wall of evil. We are caught in a psychological crossfire of anger, confusion, depression, and anxiety, as we
live with fear—the fear of ourselves or our loved ones being targeted
by the direct fire of an armed madman.

This is a time, dear friends in Christ, to fall back on faith, to let your
faith sustain you, shield you, reassure you. There is remarkable language in the selection you heard in the second reading a few moments
ago, the selection from St. Paul's Letter to the Philippians. Remember
now that without faith, Scripture is an unlighted torch. But with faith,
the word of God can enlighten and enliven you. Did this sentence in
today's second reading catch your attention? "I can do all things in him
who strengthens me" (4:13). Paul is saying, "I have the strength for
everything through him who empowers me." Try to let that idea sink
into the innermost depths of your soul. "I can do all things in him who
strengthens me."

You may feel helpless and defenseless against an insane assailant, a killer, who is on the loose, assault weapon in hand, preying on innocent men, women, and children. You may feel helpless and defenseless against terrorism on a larger scale, the type that struck the Twin Towers and the Pentagon on September 11, 2001. Helpless and defenseless only if you do not believe what Paul believed and what his inspired writing would have you personally believe, namely, that "I [you] can do all things in him who strengthens me." In that same passage Paul goes on to say: "My God will fully supply whatever you need, in accord with his glorious riches in Christ Jesus." You should be doing all you can today to unpack the "glorious riches" of that text, that scriptural promise you have as part of God's inspired word to you.

An uninspired but useful saying of a well-known liturgist, the late Sulpician Father Eugene Walsh, put that promise this way: "Jesus promises you two things: your life will have meaning and you are going to live forever. If you can find a better offer, take it!" Your life does indeed have meaning in Christ. You are destined to live forever with Christ. These are elements of the reality that Paul had in mind when he wrote to the Philippians (and derivatively to you): "My God will fully supply whatever you need, in accord with his glorious riches in Christ Jesus." Whatever you need!

Of course, we must be realistic. People do die. People are victims of accidents and assailants. It could happen to any one of us. We are all limited and frail; we are vulnerable and at risk. But our vulnerabilities and fragilities are passing things, not insignificant or trivial by any means, but passing nonetheless. We are part of something bigger than the universe where we live. We are part of Christ and can therefore say with confidence, "I can do all things in him who strengthens me."

I can do all things that he would have me do. I can reach all heights that he would have me reach. I can touch all the stars that he would have me touch. "My God will fully supply whatever [I] need, in accord with his glorious riches in Christ Jesus." Not in accord necessarily with my preferences and desires, not necessarily in accord with my self-enclosed self-interest, but in accord with the promises that are mine in Christ Jesus.

The permissive will of our Triune God will mysteriously permit evil to take its toll of human lives. The permissive will of our Triune God will mysteriously permit disease to take its toll, poverty to assault human dignity, hunger to diminish human lives. God permits these evils for reasons we cannot fathom, but God does not directly, positively will them. God permits them only because preventing them would mean overriding the freedom that belongs to human nature— free will, free choice, the freedom to choose badly, the freedom to do evil. If that freedom were removed from us, we would no longer be human. The mystery of it all is that we can use our human freedom to act in subhuman, inhuman ways.

But God's positive will for you and me is happiness, joy, security. Elsewhere, in Galatians 5:22, St. Paul describes God's gift of freedom to each one of us in the Holy Spirit in these very understandable terms. With the Spirit, there come to you love, joy, peace, patience, kindness, generosity, faithfulness, gentleness, and self-control. These add up to what Paul calls the "fruit" of the Spirit. These are also an outline of what life on this earth can be like for those who love the Lord, follow his will, and keep his commandments. Moreover, these characteristics name for you the streets of heaven, they give you a set of plans for the home prepared for those who love God, the place where innocent victims of evil assaults will find eternal safety and security.

All of this is there for you, all part of God's "glorious riches in Christ Jesus" that is yours. All you have to do is believe, and in that belief, say with St. Paul, "I can do all things in him who strengthens me."

Let me end with a suggestion. You may indeed be stressed, anxious, and afraid. Read the book by Scott Simon about Jackie Robinson, the first African-American to play major league baseball. Jackie Robinson was more than a bit stressed and anxious when he began playing for the Brooklyn Dodgers in 1947. Racial epithets and death threats came his way daily as he moved from city to city playing for the Dodgers. Scott Simon calls him a hero because he went about his business with calm and grace even though he had a bull's-eye on his back. The threats on his life were real. Jackie Robinson not only had to keep his eye on the ball, he had literally to keep an eye out for a rifle in the grandstands. The book, *Jackie Robinson and the Integration of Baseball*, will be a pleasant distraction in these days of anxiety; it will also remind you that doing business as usual in stressful times can be a quiet form of heroism of which, I would want to say, each one of you is surely capable.

60

Twenty-Ninth Sunday of the Year

Isaiah 45:1, 4–6; Psalm 96; 1 Thessalonians 1:1–5; Matthew 22:15–21

"REPAY TO CAESAR WHAT BELONGS TO CAESAR, AND TO GOD WHAT BELONGS TO GOD"

Today's Gospel ends on a very familiar note, one that is invoked annually at election time, and one that is generally not all that well understood. "Repay to Caesar what belongs to Caesar, and to God what belongs to God." How do you understand that?

Some will say this is the biblical basis for what is often called the "separation of church and state." That negative notion found its way into our American discourse when Roger Williams spoke in 1644 of a "wall of separation" between church and state and Thomas Jefferson picked up both the metaphor and the idea many years later.

This notion of separation of church and state has no home in the U.S. Constitution, although many think it does. The famous First Amendment to the Constitution states that Congress may not enact a law that would serve to "establish" a church in America and, as such, this is correctly referred to as the "non-establishment" or, simply "establishment" clause. This is part of our constitutional tradition here in the United States, part of who we are. We have no established church, no established religion. The question, however, inevitably comes up: "What amounts to establishment?" Or, to put it another way, what, in fact, is constitutionally impermissible when it comes to the federal government relating to religion?

Does state aid to private religious schools amount to "establishment" of religion? Does government assistance to church-related social welfare activities amount to an "establishment" of a church?

It is more accurate to speak of a "distinction" between church and state, rather than a separation. Moreover, there is surely no separation of church and society, nor was there ever intended to be here in the United States. The Church is an important part of our society. The Catholic Church is America is happy to enjoy its constitutionally guaranteed right to the free exercise of religious conviction. Religious freedom is one of the things that makes this a great country; it is one of the reasons historically why some Catholics are here.

In today's Gospel where you find the Pharisees trying to plot "how they might entrap Jesus in speech," you see the question of taxation crop up. "Is it lawful to pay the census tax to Caesar or not?" In effect, they are asking, would the followers of Jesus compromise their allegiance to him, the head of a religious movement, by paying taxes to the emperor, the head of state? Jesus can see through the question to their bad intention. "Why are you testing me, you hypocrites?" He tended not to mince words. He surely wasn't going to walk into that trap.

So he then asked them to give him a coin that would be used to pay the tax. In order to make an important point, he holds it up before them and asks them to identify the person whose image appears on the coin. They, of course, reply that it is the image of Caesar. And Jesus goes on to lay out a practical guideline, a simple principle: Give to Caesar what is his due, and give to God what is his due. In effect, he is saying that his followers are citizens of both the City of God and the City of Man. They have a dual citizenship with corresponding rights and obligations in both orders of their existence.

They pay their taxes and they enjoy their religious freedom. Many of them, out of religious conviction, educate their young, feed the hungry, care for the sick and elderly, and assist the poor. They wonder, at times, why they have to do these good works—educational and social works, the work of any good citizen—without financial assistance from the state. They are loyal to the state. How might the state be permitted to show its loyalty to them?

This is where the question arises of whether or not financial assistance from state to church would amount to the "establishment" of religion. If the courts decide that it does, then tax-paying Catholics will bear the expense of supporting their Church's good works without state aid. But that is no reason for them not to continue to petition for aid and to make their case for state assistance known.

There is another dimension of the render unto Caesar aspect of Catholic life that is often the basis of misunderstanding and controversy; this comes under the label of the "Church and politics." Wisdom and discretion are needed to keep the Church's altogether justifiable and totally defensible social justice agenda separate from partisan politics, indeed separate from all inappropriate political activity. There's the word—"inappropriate."

Both "appropriate" and "inappropriate" imply the presence or absence of judgment, experience, prudence, fairness, integrity, and a host of other qualities that are part of our religious tradition. These are qualities that can serve either to prompt action in the public square or to prompt restraint from public action on the part of the Church. The Church should indeed be involved in politics, but not in a partisan way. The cry for justice should be heard from the pulpit, but not instruction on how to vote. Morality should be preached, but in most cases not legislated. In our pluralistic society, the Church has no right to impose its views on unwilling and unbelieving others.

Carefully reasoned and deeply held moral convictions may or may not be appropriate matters for legislative action. In a representative democracy, Caesar, who rules by the will of the people, can make prudential judgments about what is or is not an appropriate inclusion in statutes related to crime and punishment. Catholic citizens have the right, in a representative democracy, to express their convictions clearly and persuasively to Caesar, and they can surely reinforce their arguments by giving or withholding their votes. But Caesar, for his part, might be forgiven on occasion for asking Catholic leaders why, if certain matters are of such great moral urgency, they are not doing a better job of instructing their own followers in the moral doctrine of their Church. If they cannot effectively teach it, can Caesar be expected to legislate it? Or, as Caesar might fairly say, if religious leaders were successful in meeting their responsibilities in the area of moral formation, there would be no need for legislation relative to some of these vexing moral issues.

And to pursue this line of thought just a bit further, if Caesar happens to be a Catholic holding elective office as president, governor, or member of Congress in our representative democracy, or is appointed to a cabinet-level position, who has the right to sit in moral judgment on his or her political decisions? Church authorities or Church members surely have the right to disagree and to make their disagreements known. But do they have a right publicly to condemn? Or, as has happened in recent years, do bishops or clergy have the right to bar a Catholic Caesar from reception of Holy Communion when the elected or appointed official presents him- or herself to receive the sacrament?

The question of scandal is not a simple one. Technically, giving scandal means inducing or encouraging another to sin. When the Communion rail becomes a battle line over which some political differences are fought out publicly, one might wonder where the scandal really lies.

Give to Caesar what is Caesar's, and to God what is God's. Jesus quite obviously had regard for God, but he also had regard for Caesar. And so must we. This means that each of us has an obligation to be alert to what is happening in the public square. Our citizenship in the City of God imposes upon us an obligation to be responsible in the City of Man. Not the least of these responsibilities, when the secular city is a representative democracy, is our obligation to register and vote. Far too few Catholics recognize this as a moral obligation.

As I said, there is a distinction between church and state, and certainly there is no separation of church from society. When all is not well in society, our religious commitment impels us to do something. This question, however, is always there to be pondered and responded to: what is appropriate and inappropriate action on the part of the person of strong religious convictions in the realm of politics?

61

Thirtieth Sunday of the Year

Exodus 22:20–26; Psalm 18; 1 Thessalonians 1:5c–10;
Matthew 22:34–40

THE GREATEST COMMANDMENT

Gratitude is brimming over in our hearts as we come to the altar this Sunday morning. We always come here to express our gratitude, to give praise and thanks to God, but today we are especially grateful that the reign of sniper terror is over in our community (Washington, DC, October 27, 2002), that our children are free to be themselves, that the suspected killers are in custody, and that we are back again to normal (whatever normal may be in these challenging times!). But grateful we are.

We are also sad with news of the death of Senator Paul Wellstone and his wife, daughter, campaign staff members, and the pilots of the Beechcraft that crashed last Friday. Death and illness touch our parish family as our weekly prayer of the faithful reminds us. So there is always good reason to be sad, but today, after three anxious weeks while an unknown killer was at work in our community, we have reason to be profoundly grateful and even more reason to hope in Christ Jesus our Lord.

Our Lord speaks to us today in familiar words from the Gospel of Matthew. You know the scene. A Pharisee—one of those rigid, letter-of-the-law types— questions Jesus ("tests" him, says Matthew), by asking: "Teacher, which commandment in the law is the greatest?" Now notice: the question focuses on the law—"which commandment in the law" is the greatest? The question comes from a stickler for the law and is directed to a teacher of the law, a rabbi. "Teacher, which commandment in the law is the greatest?"

And Jesus answers by quoting the law, the Old Law as expressed in the Book of Deuteronomy: "You shall love the Lord, your God, with all your heart, with all your soul, and with all your mind. This is the greatest and the first commandment."

Make special note of the fact, dear friends, that this is the first commandment of the *Old* Law. And Jesus goes on to say, "The second is like it: You shall love your neighbor as yourself." The entire Old Law, the law of the prophets and the rabbis is summed up in those two commandments.

"Well I try," you might say. "I try; I do my best to live up to these commandments. I try to love God with all my mind, heart, and soul; and I really try to love my neighbor as myself." Good for you. Keep trying. But don't rest on your spiritual oars just because you are doing your best to keep the Old Law.

Recall that Jesus the priest, at the Last Supper, speaking as high priest of the New Law, the New Covenant, not as a rabbi teaching the Old Law, gave us a New Commandment, a New Commandment of Love that raises the bar for all of us who call ourselves Christian. "By this will all men and women know that you are my disciples," Jesus said at the Last Supper on the night before he died, "that you have love for one another." Love one another, he said, "as I have loved you." As I have loved you. Not as you love yourself, but as I have loved you. That means, of course, loving your neighbor to the point of laying down your life for your neighbor. And if you're wondering who your neighbor is, recall the story of the Good Samaritan. Your "neighbor" is often someone who lives nowhere near your neighborhood! But your "neighbor," in this biblical sense, is also the person who lives within the walls of your own home.

The New Commandment raises the bar. An ethic of reciprocity, a Golden Rule ethic (do unto others as you would have them do unto you; love your neighbor as you love yourself) is no longer adequate. Jesus calls us to an ethic of renunciation. Love your neighbor as Christ loves you, and he, of course, showed his love for you by laying down his life for you. That's the kind of renunciation to which you, as a Christian, are called. How are we doing on that score?

Gratitude, the kind of gratitude that we feel in our hearts today after three weeks of fear, anxiety, and a painful sense of our own vulnerability, gratitude, I say, can lift us up to a level where we can face up to our obligations under the New Law, the obligation to love our neighbor, as Christ loved us, the obligation to forgive our enemies, as Christ forgave his.

Another way of speaking of your love for another is to say you "care" for that other. In the aftermath of the sniper terror that we have all experienced, let me suggest that we mull over in our minds the notion of caring for others, caring about others, caring as Christ cared and continues to care for you.

Think of those who lost their lives in the sniper shooting. Care enough about them to remember their names: James D. Martin, 55; James L. "Sonny" Buchanan, 39; Premkumar A. Walekar, 54; Sarah Ramos, 34; Lori Lewis Rivera, 25; Pascal Charlot, 72; Dean Harold Myers, 53; Kenneth Bridges, 53; Linda Franklin, 47; Conrad E. Johnson, 35. Care enough about them to remember them in your prayers as you pray for the loved ones they have left behind. Care enough to pray for the wounded who still live; pray for their return to health.

Care enough about the suspected killers to remember their names—John Allen Muhammad and John Lee Malvo—and pray for their salvation, their ultimate well-being.

In caring for others as Christ cared for you, think of the fragility of life and the foolishness of our failures to express our love to others, our failure to thank, our refusal to forgive. You heard the ages of those who died. Locate yourself in that group. If your life had been taken, is there anyone that would have been left behind who might not have heard from you a recent word of love, of thanks, of forgiveness? "Better open reproof than voiceless love," says the Book of Proverbs. Don't let your love for others in the family be voiceless. Speak to your family; speak to your neighbors. Care for them now, as Christ cared for you. Begin to care anew by saying now, what you would surely wish you would have said before, had a sniper's bullet deprived you of the opportunity to say it now. Thank God no bullet came your way; your life has been preserved. Thank God you have the continuing opportunity now to care, to care for others as Christ cared and continues to care for you.

Care about your world in a new way now. God saw that it was good when he created it, take a fresh look now and see how good this world is and how good the people around you—your neighbors—are. So many of them are in need. Think about the need for eldercare, child-care, and all the caring needs in between. You can meet a few of them. Responsibility for the care of the entire world does not rest on your shoulders; just care for one or two, every day, every week of the year. A caring note, a caring visit, a caring phone call, a caring presence of yourself, a caring gift of money to meet another's desperate need.

Your primary obligations to care look, for most of you, toward spouse, children, parents, and close relatives. Those obligations can be met and still leave room to your caring outreach to go beyond immediate family. How far, no one can say but you. If you care for no one, if you care about no one, if you show no care to others, how can you possibly say that you are living up to the New Commandment, which Christ your high priest placed on top of your preexisting obligation to love your neighbor as yourself?

We are all grateful today. Let's show our gratitude in the days and week ahead by caring for one another as Christ would have us do!

62

Thirty-First Sunday of the Year

Malachi 1:14b—2:2b, 8–10; Psalm 131;
1 Thessalonians 2:7b–9, 13; Matthew 23:1–12

"THE GREATEST AMONG YOU MUST BE YOUR SERVANT"

This is a Gospel about humility, availability, openness to service, not looking for a standing ovation whenever you do a good work, not letting recognition go to your head. "The greatest among you must be your servant," says Jesus; "Whoever exalts himself will be humbled."

I'm intrigued today by the line "Call no one on earth your father." You may prefer to gently draw my attention to the line about not seeking a place of honor at banquets, and paying attention to the saying that "whoever humbles himself will be exalted" and not the other way around. But let me stay for a moment with the notion that no one on earth should be called father.

The names we call ourselves provide perspective on how we act within any system. There's talk these days about systemic change in the Church. I wonder if anyone is thinking about change in the names we call ourselves.

I've been called "Father" for many years in this system of ordained priestly service to the Catholic community. A child, speaking of me, once asked her mother, "Whose father is he?" The mother, a young widow I had helped when her husband died in an automobile accident, found herself saying, "Anybody who needs one."

Some lay Catholics and not a few non-Catholics are uncomfortable with the title "Father." I'd trade it for "Pastor" in the united Church we all pray for, where Catholic priests, Lutheran pastors, and female ministers would not be separated by awkward nomenclature. Regrettably,

219

we are not even close to having to face that issue now. All "Monsignors" can relax! There is an apocryphal story told about a now deceased American cardinal who thought of himself as a "prince of the Church." Speaking to his assembled priests, he mentioned something that happened in his morning prayer. "I asked our blessed Lord this morning what should I do about this," said the cardinal, "and Our Lord replied to me, 'Your Eminence'...."

There is something of a flattening out, a de-layering, taking place in the Church today. It is not an erosion of authority. It is an emergence of humanity, human leadership, what some call "servant leadership." It's a movement of the Spirit bringing leadership and followership closer together in a community called Church. It is giving the gate to both hypocrisy and hyperbole in clerical circles.

"I am Joseph, your brother," said Joseph Cardinal Bernardin when he first met his assembled priests in their cathedral in Chicago. Not Joe, but Joseph. Many priests and some laypersons addressed him that way during his years of service to the church of Chicago. Visitors to the cemetery at St. John's, the Benedictine Monastery in Collegeville, Minnesota, walk up a path and see on the hill above, stump-like granite crosses over the graves of the monks. Carved onto the back of the crossbar is the first name only. "Michael," "Godfrey," "Robert"—strong, stark, dignified, solemn. I would not be surprised to see a gradual shift in future years from an emphasis on formal ecclesiastical titles to simple and straightforward baptismal names in letters and conversation between the faithful and those ordained to serve them from positions of authority in the Church.

There is a deeply felt need among lay Catholics to be seen and heard by those in authority in the Church. There is poignancy often in their plea for improved communication. Some few are strident and demanding, but most, if I am not misinterpreting the voices I'm hearing, are loyal and loving in their insistence on being heard. It is something like the "mounting urgency" that the stage directions expect of Emily in Thornton Wilder's *Our Town* when, toward the end of the play, she says, "O Mama, just look at me one minute as though you really saw me....Mama, just for a moment....Let's look at one another."

That's what many Catholics are saying, I believe, to their bishops today.

In a united Church, there will be, I'm sure, a "Holy Father," who will be addressed as "Your Holiness." He will, I suspect, regard himself as occupying the center of a circle, not the top of a pyramid. The Church will be seen as a circle of service, clearly recognizable as the body of Christ, where all members will be seen, heard, and in the habit of listening to one another.

Let's pray for that to happen. Meanwhile, let's each one of us incorporate into our own personal value systems the words Jesus spoke to the crowds over two thousand years ago and speaks again to us today: "The greatest among you must be your servant. Whoever exalts himself [or herself] will be humbled; but whoever humbles himself [or herself] will be exalted." That's the only kind of exaltation that should be of interest to any one of us.

63

Thirty-Second Sunday of the Year

Wisdom 6:12–16; Psalm 63; 1 Thessalonians 4:13–18;
Matthew 25:1–13

THE FOOLISH AND THE WISE

Scripture provides us today with a framework for reflection on wisdom and foolishness—the desire for wisdom and the avoidance of foolishness. Think of them as bookends: The Foolish on one side. The Wise on the other. Or think of wisdom and foolishness as forming one frame within which you can take a look at the picture of your life, at how both wisdom and foolishness interact, intertwine, compete, if you will, for center stage in the drama (you might prefer to call it comedy or tragedy) of your own existence.

Focus first on the desire for wisdom. That is what our first reading encourages you to do. "Resplendent and unfading is wisdom," says the selection you heard moments ago from the Book of Wisdom, "and she is readily perceived by those who love her, and found by those who seek her." This inspired passage personifies or anthropomorphizes wisdom. You will find her (Wisdom) "sitting by your gate." Welcome her and you "shall quickly be free from care." Wisdom "makes her own rounds, seeking those worthy of her." Wisdom meets those who seek her "with all solicitude." Think of wisdom as a quality of God, as the truth and straight thinking of God embodied within you.

In the Morning Prayer of the Church, the Divine Office, just last Thursday, we prayed: "Eternal Father, you give us life despite out guilt and even add days and years to our lives in order to bring us wisdom." How well are you doing on your growth in wisdom as the "days and years" are being added to your life?

What is wisdom? How is wisdom best understood? If you go to the dictionary, you will learn that wisdom is, among other things, a quality, "the quality of being wise." It is the "ability to judge soundly and deal sagaciously with facts, especially as they relate to life and conduct." It is "perception of the best ends and the best means." It is "discernment and judgment; discretion; sagacity."

Alright, you might say, but what is wisdom? The Book of Job will tell you that wisdom is "fear of the Lord," meaning reverence toward and being in awe of God. And Coleridge will tell you that "common sense in an uncommon degree is what the world calls wisdom." Webster's New International Dictionary will tell you that to be wise means to be "discerning and judging soundly concerning what is true and false, proper or improper; choosing the best ends [goals] and the best means [to reach those goals]". It means being "discreet" and it is opposed, of course, to "foolishness."

I'm fond of quoting St. Augustine who once remarked, "We were fooled by the wisdom of the serpent but saved by the foolishness of God." Divine wisdom is a sort of foolishness to the worldly eye, an overly generous, seeking-nothing-in-return kind of outpouring of sheer goodness and sharing of right knowledge. That's divine wisdom.

And again from the worldly viewpoint, there is a worldly wisdom that is a kind of cleverness, trickiness, putting-something-over-on-an-unsuspecting-other that goes by the name of wisdom. That's what Augustine meant when he said, "We were fooled by the wisdom of the serpent."

In setting up my opposite bookend, in framing our question today, I don't pose divine foolishness against divine wisdom. Divine foolishness helps to explain divine wisdom. I hope you will always appreciate genuine wisdom, the wisdom that is God's gift to you. Set that wisdom on one side of this consideration and over against it put foolishness in the sense of folly—foolishness in the person of a fool.

In the Upanishad, a book of Hindu wisdom sayings, you will read: "Abiding in the midst of ignorance, thinking themselves wise and learned, fools go aimlessly hither and thither, like blind led by the blind." And that, of course, echoes our own Bible where Jesus referred to the Pharisees as "blind leading the blind," and where we learn that if one blind person is led by another blind person, both fall into the ditch. To wallow in ignorance, to mistakenly consider yourself to be wise and learned, means that you are wandering "aimlessly hither and thither, like blind led by the blind." And that is a description of foolishness within which you and I can recognize ourselves from time to time. We can be rescued from our foolishness by the foolishness of God that we call grace. Grace can come to us in the form of wisdom, and wisdom is something for which we should always pray. I hope you'll pray for it today.

The story Jesus tells in today's Gospel points to one group of young women who were wise and another who were foolish, not good and bad, but wise and foolish. All ten of these young women have lamps and go out together to meet a bridegroom to escort him to the home of his bride where they would all enter together for a great wedding feast. But, as you will recall from the story, this gentleman was delayed in his arrival, so much so that five of those lamps used up all their oil. Those holding the burnt-out lamps had made inadequate provision for the oil needed to provide lamplight as night fell upon them. The wise virgins had enough oil; they were well prepared. The improvident ones had to go off some distance to try to purchase oil late at night and they returned after the doors to the wedding feast were closed and locked. They were left to stand outside; too late. The lesson of this parable? "Therefore, stay awake, for you know neither the day nor the hour." In other words, be prepared, plan ahead. Don't procrastinate. Be wise. Your foolishness can have serious consequences.

Christ our Lord has prepared an eternal wedding feast for all of us, including those of us who like to say, "I'm nobody's fool. I've got it all figured out. I can handle whatever turns up." Recall the words from the Upanishad: "Abiding in the midst of ignorance, thinking themselves wise and learned, fools go aimlessly hither and thither." Don't let your aimlessness or purposelessness detour you from the road home to heaven.

God's grace can help you put purpose in your life. You can substitute direction for aimless wanderings. Genuine wisdom is a gift God wants you to have. You just have to be wise enough to ask for it, smart enough to know that aimlessness will get you nowhere, humble enough to start identifying the right values and making them your own, lining up the goals in your life in accordance with those right values, and then being wise enough to choose the means that lead you to those goals.

Just remember, "We were fooled by the wisdom of the serpent, but we were saved by the foolishness of God." As we celebrate our salvation in this Eucharist, let's thank God for his foolish generosity toward us and ask him to give us true wisdom to light our way home to the eternal wedding feast he has prepared for all who love him.

64

Thirty-Third Sunday of the Year

Proverbs 31:10–13, 19–20, 30–31; Psalm 128;
1 Thessalonians 5:1–6; Matthew 25:14–30

USE YOUR TALENTS TO GAIN A SHARE IN YOUR MASTER'S JOY

Jesus, the storyteller, speaks to you today about talent. That word, as you know, originally meant a sum of money. So keep that fact in mind as you reflect on the parable communicated by Matthew in the selection from his Gospel that you just heard.

Matthew has Jesus recounting a story about a man who was starting out on a journey. Before he left, he called his servants together and, in the words of the Gospel, "entrusted his possessions to them [to the servants]. To one he gave five talents; to another, two; to a third, one— each according to his ability." Think about that. Each received some talent, "according to his ability," according to his capacity to receive. And think in terms of the talents you yourself have. The master in this story, surely a figure representing God, "entrusted his possessions" to these servants (to be understood as representing you and me). The Lord gave all of them talents, entrusted talents to them that belonged in fact to the Lord. "He entrusted his possessions to them." You possess talents that belong to him. Your talents are his possessions! The talents that you have belong to God. Using those talents well is one way you have of glorifying God.

The story goes on to indicate that the fellow who received five talents invested them wisely and gained five more. Similarly the one who received two invested his talents and in return received two more. And the fellow who was given one talent could have invested it, but chose not to do so. Instead, he buried it for safekeeping.

Notice how timidity enters the story here. Notice how timidity can cripple progress, stymie investment, how it can quite literally bury talent.

The master returns, as you will remember, to settle accounts. Those who took a bit of risk and invested their talents found to their surprise that they had also contributed to their "master's joy." They could keep their gain, of course, and they were rewarded with high praise and even greater responsibilities. The timid fellow who admits that "out of fear" he buried the talent in the ground, draws a sharp rebuke. Moreover he has his single talent taken from him and receives no praise but hears instead these words of rebuke: "Throw this useless servant into the darkness outside, where there will be wailing and grinding of teeth." His timidity is rewarded by darkness and bitterness. It is all so sad.

It is also so avoidable, if only he had been up for a bit of risk.

Take inventory of your own talents for a moment this morning, my brothers and sisters. To count your blessings is another way of describing what I'm asking you to do. Still another way would be to ask you to count those possessions of the Lord that he has entrusted to you, to be put to use for his glory. Be sure you first recognize that they are God's possessions, not yours. Realize as well that they as in your possession to be invested for God's glory, not yours.

Don't hide behind the mask of timidity and say you have no talents. You certainly do. You may not have developed them much over the years, but that is not to say that you cannot begin investing them now. You can walk, talk, think, smile. You can write, calculate, lend a helping hand, volunteer, reach out to others. Maybe you can sing and dance and play a musical instrument (those very narrow notions of "talent" that the so-called talent scouts notice). Maybe you have athletic or artistic talents. Perhaps you are intellectually gifted. Perhaps you are a good listener. Your talents may be most evident in the kitchen or garden. The point now, as you take your inventory, is: (1) do not permit timidity to tell that lie that you have no talent to speak of; (2) consider how you might have been neglecting or hiding the talent you have; and (3) begin right now to plan how you can use your talents for the glory of God and the good of your brothers and sisters in the human community.

In his 1990 book *Leadership*, the late John Gardner wrote: "Most men and women go through their lives using no more than a fraction—usually a rather small fraction—of the potentialities within them. The reservoir of unused human talent and energy is vast, and learning to tap that reservoir more effectively is one of the exciting tasks ahead for humankind" (p. xix).

If you fail to invest your talents (the possessions that belong to God and that have been entrusted to you), if you fail to invest, you run the very high risk of losing the talents you have and finding yourself out in the dark "wailing and grinding [your] teeth," frustrated, unfulfilled, unhappy.

Think about using your talents at home; using your talents at work, using your talents in the community, using your talents here in the parish. And if you find yourself in a box, so to speak, maybe even feeling a little frustrated because you are unable to give your talents a good stretch, take a moment of prayerful self-assessment. If illness, age, or some physical incapacity hinders your use of the talents you have, accept that and incorporate it into the sufferings that Christ accepted for the salvation of the world. Your limits can become effective when incorporated into the passion and death of Jesus; your limits can, in Christ, have redemptive power. Second, if you have simply been hesitant to take a risk and invest your talents in any new initiative, think about taking that risk now, and think of your possible need for a nudge in the direction of taking a decisive step. If that is the case, pray today to the Lord who owns your talents and has loaned them to you for appropriate management and investment, and pray for the nudge you might need to put those talents to work.

Once you start moving in that direction, you can count on your Master saying to you, as the master in this Gospel story said to his "good and faithful" servants, "Come, share in your master's joy." May every one of you hear those words from time to time and have them sink into the depths of your satisfied souls.

65

Thirty-Fourth Sunday of the Year, Solemnity of Our Lord Jesus Christ, King of the Universe

Ezekiel 34: 11–12, 15–17; Psalm 23; 1 Corinthians 15: 20–26, 28; Matthew 25:33–46

SEPARATION OF THE SHEEP FROM THE GOATS

This is the Feast of Christ the King. The Gospel story places us—the entire human race—before the throne of Christ the King in what is often called the Last Judgment. We've been pilgrims on this earth. We've heard the word of God here on earth and either acted on it or rejected it. We've been part of the community of faith known as the Church. We've lived our lives. And here we are the end of time at the moment of judgment.

We are about to be separated into two groups—one Jesus has classified as sheep and the other goats. That classification will have eternal consequences—eternal punishment for the goats, eternal life for the sheep. The stakes are high. You can imagine great tension in the air.

Too late there at the point of judgment to alter the record, to undo misdeeds, correct omissions, and put more points on the board, so to speak. No, the score has been tallied. It is final. It is now just a matter of letting the record speak for itself.

To the sheep the king will say, "Come, you who are blessed by my Father. Inherit the kingdom prepared for you from the foundation of the world."

Why, if you are so fortunate, are you lined up there with the sheep? Why will you inherit the kingdom? Because, as Jesus explained, "I was hungry and you gave me food, I was thirsty and you gave me drink. I was a stranger and you welcomed me, naked and you clothed me, ill and you cared for me, in prison and you visited me." So, my friends, see yourselves standing there. Hear Christ speaking this way about you.

You, along with the other just men and women assembled there might find yourself asking, as the just in this Gospel story asked, "Lord, when did we see you hungry and feed you, or thirsty and give you drink? When did we see you a stranger and welcome you, or naked and clothe you? When did we see you ill or in prison and visit you?" And Christ, portrayed as the king in this story, will say to you: "Whatever you did for one of the least brethren of mine, you did for me."

There are sobering, even frightening dimensions of this story. First, it could not be plainer or more clear that Jesus is identifying with the hungry, the poor, the imprisoned, the homeless, and the sick. He is there; he is they.

Do we see him there, can we locate him in them, in those people in need? Do we get anywhere near the places where they are—the hospitals, the prisons, the slums, the mean streets? Or, have we chosen to isolate ourselves from them and thus chosen to distance ourselves from him? These, as I say, are sobering, even frightening questions. We all have our own comfort zones, our private preserves, our security areas. This Gospel story is inviting us to step outside our safety zones in order to be able to help those in need.

It might just not be enough for us, on Judgment Day, to say we sent a check, or signed a petition, or sent a letter, or made a call, or contributed to the food drive. It might not be enough to have passed the hat, so to speak, without reaching out and touching the needy person. I'm not saying those failures will shift you immediately over to the company of the goats; I'm saying that indirect assistance may not really be enough. So search your soul and see what you find there by way of an answer to that question.

The Gospel story goes on to tune you in to the words the king speaks to those on his left—the goats: "Depart from me you accursed, into the eternal fire prepared for the devil and his angels. For I was hungry and you gave me no food, I was thirsty and you gave me no drink, a stranger and you gave me no welcome, naked and you gave me no clothing, ill and in prison and you did care for me." Again, these are frightening words. They elicit from the hearers there on the left, from the goats, defensive queries about when they saw him in need and failed to respond, and his answer once again is clear and direct: "Amen I say to you, what you did not do for one of these least ones, you did not do for me."

How applicable is that to you? Are you guilty of neglect in the face of human hardship? The Gospel story is not accusing you of directly causing the hardship, directly inflicting harm; no, the Gospel is pointing out the danger to you of obliviousness, the negative consequences of your own neglect.

Each one of us risks becoming oblivious. The social and residential arrangements that we take for granted, the education and economic security that most of us enjoy, isolate us from the needs of others and, in a manner of speaking, insulate us from an awareness that we are obliged to help our neighbor in need. The beauty of this Gospel story is that is locates the person of Christ in the needy person; it points you into a direct relationship of love and care for Christ by explaining that Christ is there in the person in need of help and you are in direct contact with Christ when you reach out to the person in need of help.

If you want to get closer to Christ, get closer to the poor, this Gospel is saying; feed him in the poor, visit him in prison, care for and comfort him in the ill.

Probably all of us have looked the other way at times when the beggar approached; some of us may have crossed over to the other side of the street. But consider for a moment how the beggar on the street may be doing you a favor. He or she may be bringing Christ to you when you, protected as you are from direct contact with the poor by your social and economic circumstances, do not really know the poor. You don't have ready access to the poor. But there they are from time to time, on the corner, at your door, on the driver's side of your car as you stop at the traffic signal. Don't ignore them. The Gospel today is telling you that they are Jesus in disguise. Help them and you are helping him.

It takes courage and creativity on your part to put yourself in face-to-face contact with a prisoner. It may take a certain amount of resourcefulness for you to become friendly with someone who is poor. It certainly takes time and a measure of generosity to visit the sick. All that is true. But it is also true, as your Gospel message today makes clear, that your salvation depends on your desire to reach out to the poor, to prisoners, to the sick, and your willingness to translate that desire into deed in some measureable, meaningful way.

No one ever said that discipleship was going to be easy!